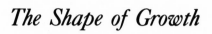

The Shape of Growth

The Shape
Of Growth

Gale D. Webbe

MOREHOUSE BARLOW
Wilton

ACKNOWLEDGEMENTS

Material in Chapters 3, 5, 8, 11, and 12 appeared in an earlier form in *The Living Church*. The author acknowledges with gratitude permission to reprint herein.

The final form of this book owes much to several readers who studied it in preliminary manuscript and made many valuable suggestions. To them all I extend my sincere appreciation.

BV
4501.2
·W414
1985

Morehouse Barlow Co., Inc.
78 Danbury Road
Wilton, Connecticut 06897

ISBN 8192-1356-X

Library of Congress Catalog Card Number 84-62357

Composition by
BSC Litho
3000 Canby Street
Harrisburg, PA 17103

Printed in the United States of America

To my wife,
with great gratitude
for fifty-five
years of encouragement.

Contents

Introduction

A PERENNIAL DIFFICULTY about "self-expression" is that it requires and assumes something of a self to be expressed. Ultimately, even the most determined free spirit is apt to become frustrated from bumping his head against this truth and sense that he is imprisoned by too much freedom, by lack of principle; that he is wandering in darkness, because he lacks a guiding light. He can glimpse the fact that selves of any consequence are produced only in a life of obedience to something outside themselves.

It is true that every now and then we are startled by a seemingly natural-born genius, who flashes into view and streaks across the sky leaving the rest of us gaping. At first glance it seems that, rarely, God can lay His hand upon a person who immediately emerges whole, entire, and single-minded. Naturally, such persons perform extremely special work in the world, which is why we notice them, and the suspicion is raised that God has prepared the ground in some extraordinary way. These exceptions even move us to toy with the concept of irresistible grace—the notion that on occasion God brushes aside human free will. However, common sense clings to the conviction that God does not play favorites and ultimately prevails over our envy. We suspect that undoubtedly even these special streams run in the usual direction; that the genius remains an example of Grace-and Response, if indeed an unusual one; and that certainly the situation with these mysterious exceptions has little to do with us ordinary people anyway. The truth with the ninety and nine of us is that proficiency, and possible excellence, come only after commitment, application, and persistence.

So I am assuming that somewhere along the line we discerned the strictures of reality, and at least grudgingly acknowledged that we are not gods but creatures. We knew, possibly in anger or even in despair initially, that we were always going to be in service to something. We saw that creaturely life means that we live in bondage—to our own selfishness; to whim, emotion, body; to the curious standards of the world around us; to the demands of our job; to the pull of our special Muse; to any of the host of obedience possibilities. We realized that since creaturely life means that we are always going to have to be obedient, the practical problem was to distinguish slavery from service. Surely the better master, the higher obedience, we chose would determine the self we would ultimately become.

Then came the dawn of hope. Perhaps life did not merely tantalize, but actually delivered on its hints? Perhaps if we chose the perfect master, and arrived at perfect obedience to him, we would then have achieved perfect human freedom? Maybe Means determine Ends just as surely as Ends determine Means?

The affirmative answer to these questions is the Christian position. We are persuaded that "God's service is perfect freedom"; that obedience and freedom are corelative, not contradictory, terms; that the disciplined obedient life is not the enemy of the creative life but its friend and enabler. (C. G. Jung agrees, saying in *Modern Man in Search of a Soul*, "It is not the children of the flesh, but the 'children of God' who know freedom.") So primary is this truth amongst us that the first thing we hear at the dawning of each new Christian Year is the Collect for St. Andrew, Christ's first disciple and hence our archetype, who "readily obeyed . . . without delay." There is good reason to say that "Obedience" is close to the best single word that can be used in describing the Christian life. Scholars tell us that in the New Testament "The Obedient" is almost a technical term denoting those united to Christ. Saints down the Christian ages chime in, proclaiming in word and deed that Christian perfection is the living linking of the human will with the will of God at every moment. The complete synchronizing of these two forces, as in "Whatsoever He saith unto you, do it," is their most widely chosen way for expressing the fruition, the achieving of the purpose of human life.

"Obedience" is a debased word in our day, however. It falls on the modern ear with a leaden thud. Perhaps its high and vibrant content can be somewhat recovered by pointing out that the saints construe perfect human obedience as consisting of our entering wholly, completely into the Obedience of Christ. They do not mean a merely external obedience *to* Him, nor any other such surface understanding of the presently unfortunate phrase, "The Imitation of Christ." Classically, "Obedience" is a much more mystical expression meaning "entering into the Obedience that was Christ's"—the Obedience of Him who took as His life's motto "Lo, I come to do Thy will, O God", and whose work was to gather the whole fallen creation back into that Obedience. They see that all manner of things will ultimately be well, because the Obedience our Lord achieved for us as our representative will finally be achieved in us. They really mean that each of us will attain his life's desire, will come to his own perfect being, in Christ. Here again, they are at one with the New Testament, which wholly glows with this same realization that the Christian life is a personal participation in the Obedience that Christ lived.

It is important to note that the witness in the New Testament and in the lives of the saints is not a matter of theory but of practice; not a wistful hope about the nature and possibility of human life but a shout of conviction. The testimony that "real life" has actually been lived in human circumstances indicates that it can be lived by you and me, if we go about it properly. This book addresses itself to certain practical matters connected with the living of that life—the "spiritual life" as it is called. It investigates some of the tried and true means in that life, expressed in "Episcopalian" language (like the references to "each new Christian Year" and "the Collect for St. Andrew"), because that is the language of the writer. It is simply my unfamiliarity with the spiritual treasury of religious traditions other than my own that inhibits my speaking in their native tongues to all travelers on the way. However, the discussion herein centers on universal verities and practices rather than on their particular expressions, and I am confident that it should not be difficult, when necessary, to translate from my terminology into one's own familiar expression of the same truth.

The scope of the discussion is, I trust, complete enough to offer practical guidance in one's spiritual development toward selfhood and self-expression, but this brief book by no means attempts to offer a thorough exposition of the spiritual life, such as F. P. Harton has made available in his classic *The Elements of the Spiritual Life*. Nor does it try to present completely, even on a beginning level, that part of the spiritual life which we call prayer. (Again there is no loss; among others, Constance Garrett has done this well in her *Growth in Prayer*.) I have confined myself closely within the limits of the purpose stated and have assumed that the reader has had spiritual experience.

Some other obvious assumptions are made herein, including the rather moot question of "religious authority." I am aware that we live in a crumbling society where inevitably much is being made of crumbling authorities. In our era we have once again exercised mankind's talent for destroying its own fun—for killing God—and once again we stand aghast at the failure of our success. The classic guideposts lie in scattered ruin around us, and nobody can tell us exactly which way to turn. The Bible, the Church, traditional morality, the concept of revelation, the historic creeds, the Christian consensus down the ages—all are out of court nowadays, along with traditional secular standards. We seem to be left with "personal experience," which is running its usual course from despair to delirium and back again. In some quarters we hear the boast, "I can call spirits from the vasty deep!"

The classic response to that, of course, is "Well, so can I, and so can any man—but will they come?" This may seem a mocking retort, even a thumbing of the nose, but I think that our present situation is really fine, at bottom, because each new generation understandably feels it must make trial of madness before it is content to return to sanity. I am quite confident that ours will, and be the better for it.

The discerning reader will perceive that my own authority, or Ariadne's thread, really is "the Christian consensus." In a broader sense, it is "that which has been tried in wide experience by the sanctified common sense of our brothers and sisters and found not wanting." In fact it has been found glorious, and I do believe that every "personal experience" will validate once again the universal miracle that by entering into the Obedience of Christ we do become our perfect selves. So, in a way, I do not think that "the moot problem of authority" is really that important after all. God really is alive, His universe is orderly, He craves to enter into our beings and our doings, and so the final authority always resides safely in human living itself. I have a blithe confidence that ultimately we can always rest our case upon the existential "taste and see," or "come on in, the water's fine."

Chapter One

Conversion

THE DESIRE and the search for the Invisible Infinite is the bittersweet lot of the human race, whose insatiable longing is that the Absolute may be attained, the End arrived at, the Altogether Lovely held in permanent embrace. At the time of our conversion we glimpse this far-off vision with peculiar clarity, and our significant history begins. We then touch authenticity, at however long remove, and there is created in us a permanent nostalgia for home.

"Conversion," unfortunately, is a good word that has suffered much; a faithful old servant that has been grievously wounded in the house of its friends. A decent respect for the feelings of mankind makes us hesitate to reintroduce it, all torn and bleeding as it is, to polite society. Respect for the word itself urges us to grant it a richly earned retirement. Respect for the eternal verities, however, forces us to send "conversion" back to its duties again, first having washed its face and bound up its wounds.

The word, even when used in its technical religious sense, simply means the "turning around," the reorientation of the whole person, that its etymology suggests. In itself it is a perfectly harmless expression. In fact it would be hard to coin a better word to describe the fateful awakening in which a soul faces away from his past and looks toward a different future. It needs cosmetic treatment first of all, because earnest folk, consumingly aware of the enormous significance of their own turning, have made the zealot's typical error of generalizing from the limited basis of personal experience. They have added unwarranted modifiers such as "violent," "gentle," "slow," "sudden," "emotional," "intellectual," "volitional," "grudging," "generous," "fearful," "loving," and many more.

The fact is that conversion experiences, many of which are not even experienced save in retrospect, are as infinitely varied as humankind itself. To each his own. Suffice it that in the beginning all souls are without form and void; darkness is upon the face of their deep. In His own time and manner the Spirit of God moves upon the face of the waters, blowing as He listeth. It is quite impossible to say what form any turning will take.

It is equally impossible to assert definitely what will prompt a particular conversion. Certainly no human can produce it. Conversion is of God. Necessarily acting, in this sacramental world, through some combination of circumstances peculiarly adapted to each individual, God gives us a glimpse of the real possibilities of life at His own prepared moment. With sufficient clarity we then know, each in our own way, that time is given to us so that we may enter into eternity. Speaking negatively, at conversion we know dissatisfaction with the obvious. Speaking positively, we then long for reality. The heart begins its hunger for home.

Conversion is a brief awakening, a flickering of the spiritual eyelids, an awareness, a turning; there is no movement in it save a circular one by which one sees a new horizon. Like its obvious natural parallel, being born—which also occurs without our having been consulted on the matter—it produces nothing except infinite possibility. Like waking up, it does not guarantee that we shall immediately rise and begin a purposeful day. One can easily close one's eyes, turn back again, and go to sleep. Without affirmative response from human free will, even omnipotent God has to take "no" for an answer. Herein lies a second reason why "conversion" has fallen on evil days. Some "born again" people, in their most understandable enthusiasm, give the impression that in their thinking a conversion event outranks and even makes unnecessary a long consequent process of sanctification. In actuality they know, perhaps better than most, that the facts of the matter are quite otherwise—a point to be addressed in brief shortly, and at length throughout this whole book. Nevertheless a suspicion has been raised, and the damage has been done.

The writer is convinced that every living soul comes to his moment of truth, or conversion opportunity. My dogmatism is, obviously, not based upon intimate personal acquaintance with the billions of souls now populating the earth, much less with the vast army that has existed since the arrival of *homo sapiens*. Nor is it based on our Lord's "many are called," although it is comforting to have His assessment on the subject. The conviction really rests upon the assumptions that the universe makes sense and that the overall purpose of creation is to produce personality on its highest possible level of consciousness. (These highly likely hypotheses are, of course, fundamentally unprovable. However, they make human life so purposeful that it would seem worthwhile to accept them even if we knew, with certainty, that they were merely wishful thinking and utterly false.)

The God of such a universe would, inevitably, find ways to let His sentient creatures know that they are eternal souls doing time. That in the "conversion experience" He does in fact do so seems abundantly clear. Converts who are analytically inclined will testify that involved in our awakening is sufficiently clear discernment of the true psychology of man. We then know we are amphibians, creatures of two worlds, torn between a downdrag and an upward pull. There may even be some apprehension of the truth in St. Ignatius's words:

"In a bad man, evil tries to keep him in peace; good tries to raise him to anxiety. In a good man, bad tries to rouse anxiety, good to keep him in peace." In any case, we turn from the one world to the other precisely because we know that Nature is not all there is.

In some conversions the sense of "otherness", of intrusion into nature from outside, is markedly strong. In others, only later rumination concludes that God can and occasionally does slip or burst into this world, because manifestly He has done so in their case. With varying degrees of intensity, however, conversion brings assurance of a "call" or vocation from God. The last person on earth to take that statement in a literal sense would, usually, be the convert himself. He hears no voice. Nevertheless he knows in his heart that it was not of himself that "he came to himself."

He also knows that "self" is the wrong word to use in describing the mere jumble of potentiality he is at the moment. His vocation is to become a self. He sees that if he responds to the call he will engage in a creative process toward a far-off goal and thus fulfill the purpose of life.

Both fortunately and unfortunately, he has little awareness of how hard and how slow that process will be. Since he has no real idea of the difficulties in the path he will be treading, he does not know how strong must be his initial resolution to move forward. The ignorance has its good side, however, in that the words "duty," "obedience," "discipline" do not, at conversion, seem forbidding. A sincere convert views them with joy. He wants them. He anticipates them as eagerly as an aspirant for athletic glory looks forward to his hot and dusty practice sessions. For the joy that is set before him, he actually desires to pick up his cross. He knows quite well that vision, far from making drill, drudgery, and detail nonexistent, makes these elements both necessary and worthwhile.

Therefore any once-over-lightly Confirmation instruction, with little or no reference to spiritual discipline and rule, is not merely insulting. It is a devastating dash of cold water. Converts, typically, understand quite well that in Christianity God has called and destined the human race to the most glorious through the most arduous. Beyond that, converts demonstrate a "disinterestedness" amazing in its purity when one considers that the chief struggle later on will be to perfect this element above all. At conversion we discern God as deserving of the absolute best, and we intend to give it to Him. A resolution to develop, with God's help, the most extremely delicate modes of perception possible to us is then in some degree undertaken more for God's glory than for our own, to state this in terms the neophyte would not understand. Yet his new life is *devoted*, in the strict sense of that word, with desire that the purpose of the universe be achieved, again to use an expression foreign to the beginner.

Perhaps most importantly, down in the depths of our inarticulate beings, we make at conversion the fundamental choice as to the ultimate End of Man. We "would not live that which is not life, living is so dear"; we know that ends determine means, and we decide that the End of Man is the Vision of God. We make the historic "mystic" choice that the soul was created for aspiration toward, and attainment of, the Good, the Beautiful, and the True.

Many students have observed the human scene and have drawn the charitable conclusion that God does not, indeed, awaken everyone. Right or wrong, they help us answer the question, "If only God can induce conversion, why then do you stress the event so strongly?"

The answer stems from evidence that conversion is a fragile and a transitory thing. It is a tender plant thrusting up through hard crust into a bleak and, in many ways, hostile climate—a "fallen" world. With careful cultivation it will, without any question, grow and flourish. Untended, however, it will almost surely wither and die.

One must seize the opportunity. Conversion is indeed absolutely pivotal—the essential beginning of the spiritual life—because it is an energized packet of vision and motivation, of desire and zeal. (There are those who say that all the troubles of the Church result from so many of its members being unconverted. The diagnosis covers a multitude of sins but may well be right.) Nevertheless, a lifelong process of interaction between grace and response must begin and continue, if we are to become one with the initially glimpsed reality. The chapters that follow will sketch some time-tested methods of fruitful response, perforce chosen mainly from the spiritual treasury of the Anglican Communion. Saints by the score justify the claim that, with the use of these resources, the human dream can be realized in a most adequate manner—indeed, that one will ultimately be granted the Vision of God.

Yet we cannot leave the subject of conversion without pointing out that so far we have considered it only as an initiating event. We have been discussing the First Conversion. It is important to make clear that much later, after long progress in the spiritual life, we experience the Second Conversion. Then, but not until then, the fundamental human problem—the problem of the double will, of strong attraction to both worlds—will be resolved.

In short, the spiritual birth of First Conversion initiates a process in which the soul moves toward the vision then glimpsed. It energizes us to fight through the thickets and brambles of the foothills. When we burst out, scarred and battered, lean and tempered, we only stand at the foot of the mountain itself. At this point a spiritual "second wind" enables the now unwavering soul to begin the real climb, up through the swirling mists and thick darkness where God really is.

Chapter Two

Diagrams

THE JOURNEY THROUGH time to eternity, through Becoming to Being, is in its details different for each traveler. "There is no expeditious road, To pack and label men for God, And save them by the barrel-load." (Francis Thompson, *Epilogue, A Judgement in Heaven*). The Spirit blows where, when, and how He wills, and God meets each person according to the individuality of that person. We all have noticed how, in the Resurrection appearances of the first Easter, our Lord came to each disciple in a manner adapted to that disciple's need at the moment—with triple forgiveness to Peter of the triple denial; with dispelling proof to doubting Thomas. He still does.

From our own side in this intensely personal matter, we do the same with God. We approach Him as we are and from where we are. We company with Him in our individual way. Just as on a golf course we all play the same game in personal style or with individual awkwardness, so on the far more subtle spiritual course there are temperamental differences and varying natural gifts. Some people have ten talents, others have five, and many of us have only one.

Nevertheless, there is a general pattern in the personal relationship with God. There is a basic spirituality for all, because the End—God—is the same yesterday, today, and forever; and all of us infinitely varying individuals are, at bottom, members of the same species. Hence our passage is, in broad essentials, the same for all. Everyone enters from stage left, as it were; gropes around for a while in the pitiless glare of the spotlight, shading his eyes so that he may distinguish a few gross shapes; and then is summoned off into the darkness at stage right. Since the solid beginnings and continuings of the spiritual life are of one general pattern for all, they can indeed be systematically expressed—can be taught and learned somewhat like the alphabet and the parts of speech. Our Lord acted thus with His diverse disciples. When they reached a certain point and said, "Lord, teach us to pray," He did so, to the group. He still does, through His new body, the Church. Earnestly seeking people can confidently come to it for the furthering and enabling of their individual spiritual lives in its corporate life. There is no need to turn to the esoteric and the occult, much less to psychedelic drugs, in the search for God. The Church has, sometimes hidden under a bushel, what they are looking for.

We have already indicated that we will be investigating some of these means, which came from Him and which lead to Him. Before examining particular techniques, however, it will be best to scan the spiritual life as a whole. Applications are impossible without principles. Particular matters like corporate worship and private prayer; like praise, thanksgiving, intercession, and all the rest; like retreats and quiet days; like Schools of Prayer and the Stations of the Cross; like fasting and receiving sacraments; take their rise from, find their place in, and contribute to the whole.

Again, because of these fundamental similarities among all the diverse travelers on the road, the general outline of Everyman's spiritual journey can be adequately charted, and it has been. Some of those who have made the trip had a gift for cartography and have left us maps leading to the goal. It is heartening that all of these maps—some quite simple, others enormously detailed, many of them drawn up independently of the rest and even without reference to them—agree in the essentials. This suggestion of their accuracy is reinforced by their conformity to truth as we ourselves have glimpsed it. Heart does speak to heart when we study these diagrams, and that is always the surest authority we can know.

The simplest map, leading from where we are to where we want to be, sketches an ascending trail on three levels called The Purgative Way, The Illuminative Way, and The Unitive Way. This description has its deficiencies, but fruitful discussion of the developing spiritual life remains impossible without reference to the classic triad.

For that matter, analysis of development in any dynamic area reveals the identical, the inevitable, outline. Purgation . . . Illumination . . . Union is the very 'shape' of all growth. Every Boy Scout leader knows the structure well, from his experience with Tenderfoot, Second Class, and First Class levels of proficiency; so does every parent, every athletic coach, every English teacher.

The latter, to take an example illustrating all, desires about everything else that her students reach the point from which they can freely roam, with full appreciation and an ache in their throats, through the entire field of classic English literature. She hopes, indeed, that some of them will one day make their own contributions to the undying corpus. On the road to that sublime end she first submits her charges to a purgative necessity—strict drill in grammar, punctuation, and vocabulary. A little later, as illumination dawns, she begins to allow and to urge some freedom in composition and interpretation. Union, it should be noted, is not really hers to give. She can only share it with great joy, if and when it is arrived at, entered upon, and bestowed rather from without, as it were by the spirit of the thing.

The growing spiritual life progresses along the same broad familiar trail. We follow this Way to the Truth and the Life. We begin in clumsy servanthood,

9

subsequently move to more relaxed friendship, and then one glorious day finally realize that all along we really have been beloved sons.

In greater detail swiftly stated, characteristic of The Purgative Way is the sense of being a servant of God, to whom one is bound by a rather remote loyalty. The inner self is fragmented, and the spiritual regime is dominated by activities that seek to discipline the inner chaos. Despite a merely surface self-knowledge, there is "general" penitence for a whole host of particular shortcomings, specific self-denials with the same goal in view, and the diligent cultivation of good habits in the trust that they will make life smoother. These habits naturally include prayer, which is predominately vocal and generally practiced by "saying prayers." The characteristic mental prayer is discursive meditation.

In the Illuminative Way one has become aware, quite truly, that one is a friend of God, enjoying the bonds of comradeship. The "self" is growing worthy of that name and hence enjoying considerable freedom, while at the same time constituting an entity that can be and is denied. Such denial follows inevitably upon the greater degree of self-knowledge that has become available, and the connected truth that motives, rather than sheer actions, are looming in importance. "Particular" penitence, which ferrets out a besetting sin and its temptations deep in the ground of one's being, accompanies the shift. There is a growing love of solitude and silence, a sincere desire to imitate Christ, and a considerable degree of spiritual suffering. (For a study of problems and pains that arise in the more mature spiritual life see my book *The Night and Nothing*, Harper & Row, 1983.) Typically, one has moved through "affective" prayer to contemplation, and the prayer-life has experienced much real aridity.

On the other side of that pain and dryness, one enters into the Unitive Way where one humbly knows oneself to be a son of God, bound to his Father by the warmest love and abandoned to Him in complete trust. His selfhood is attained, his life simple, his character stable, his detachment complete, his "channel" clear, and therefore his creativity high. Recollection is a constant state, and he has been granted high levels of the Prayer of Union.

The following list of characteristics, arranged in rough parallels or progressions from Purgation through Union, may help to clarify the matter.

Purgative	*Illuminative*	*Unitive*
Servants	Friends	Sons
Loyalty	Comradeship	Love
Habit	Freedom	Creativity
Self-Denial	Denial of Self	Abandonment
Actions	Motives	Simplicity
Meditation	Contemplation	Union
"General" Penitence	"Particular" Penitence	Acceptance
Fragmentation	Double-Mindedness	Selfhood
Activity	Quiet	Recollection
"Morality"	Imitation of Christ	Stability

It is important to note that the above analysis does not attempt to be complete, or even wholly accurate. Its main purpose is to illustrate the Ways in general and the progression in particular. As a matter of fact, it is probably impossible to characterize any one Way completely and certainly impossible to do so exclusively. There are no sharp edges between Purgation, Illumination, and Union. One stage merges into the other. Each shares something of what went before, and even of what comes after. Growth is a fluid and uneven thing, more like the inflow of the tide than the rising of the sun or, to change the figure, it resembles toiling up an undulating slope more than it does climbing stairs. We point this out, not with any view to confuse, but to underline the warning that it is always unhealthy to "scratch at one's soul"—in the present connection, to introspect continually in the forlorn attempt to discover precisely what Way one is "in." It is not only centipedes that become immobilized by worrying about the proper order for moving their legs.

Nevertheless, the classic description has its enormous values. It may be especially important to recall it in an era that tends to ignore the Purgative Way in religion altogether, perhaps forgetting that the higher always depends for its support upon the lower. The practical question, always, is "*How* do we achieve selfhood?" How do we arrive at that lovely Unitive state? Not by any "religionless Christianity," if that loose phrase has any real meaning at all. I experienced a neat parable of this on a jet airplane that, from the moment of takeoff, had to batter its way aloft through extremely rough air. During the long climb I was reading a sermon entitled "The Yoke of Christ," in which Dr. Tillich, its author, urges that Christ came to break the heavy yoke of previous religion—indeed to destroy 'religion,' in one sense of that word. In compelling words, Tillich called us all to a high free way of life fully worthy of the risen Lord.

I finished the sermon just as we broke into the serenity of the 30,000 feet-plus altitude. Beside me my companion sighed, loosened her seat belt, and said, "My, it's nice to be up here in the smoothness. What always gets me is the shaking-up process through which we arrive. But then, of course we do have to go through all that."

I put Dr. Tillich away. I thought she had him there.

Tracing spiritual growth by way of Purgative . . . Illuminative . . . Unitive stages does have many deficiencies. It is so compressed a description that it lacks a beginning (conversion) and, what is even more serious, has a gaping hole in it (the Second Conversion). It gives the impression of a straight-line progression, such as Horatio Alger's heroes made from rags to riches by dint of sheer diligent hard work, and thus suggests the deceiving half-truth that "practice makes perfect." Hence it implies a static, pre-depth-psychology view of human personality that can leave a person disastrously unprepared when he finds himself caught up in life's enormous dynamic.

Another analysis of the developing spiritual life takes full account of that dynamic. This is a four-stage framework, conforming to the familiar Fourfold Shape of the Liturgy—"He took, He blessed, He brake, He gave"—which diagrams the action at the Last Supper. ("For in the night in which He was betrayed He took bread, and when He had given thanks He brake it, and gave it to them.") The same fourfold structure is found in Christ's Feedings of the Multitudes, where "He took the loaves, and gave thanks, and brake, and gave to His disciples to set before them." Herein is one of the greatest parables, or paradigms, of Divine-human interaction in all its true dynamism.

1.—"He took." At the time of our conversion we give ourselves, or something of ourselves, to God. When we offer Him these few loaves and fishes, this tentative consent of our will, we are saying the all-important "Yes" of human free will to the promptings of prevenient God. All joyfully, "He takes" what we have placed at His disposal. A bridge drops down, affording creative contact between that land and this. Anything can happen, and many things will, now that the spiritual life has started. (Conversion remains the terribly important matter that was sketched in the opening chapter, as does the definite beginning of a vertical "I-Thou" relationship between God and man. So long as people remain safely on one side of a wall with God barricaded beyond it and all I-Thou kept contained on the merely horizontal level, between man and man, nothing of spiritual consequence happens.)

2.—"He blessed." Entirely overlooking the fact that our gift to Him may be hesitant, partial, soiled, calculating, or even despairing, God returns extended thanks over it. "He blesses" in astounding ways as we persevere in our beginning spiritual exercises. This period in the religious life corresponds to The Purgative Way, which is not as grindingly dull and plodding as one might imagine. There is much glory here and considerable high adventure. In this phase, for example, astonishing visible character changes are rather apt to occur—bad habits are corrected, a neurosis surmounted, a phobia broken through. In the devotional life, God's presence is often palpably near. Prayers are apt to be answered speedily, often affirmatively. Visions of one kind or another can occur. Out in the larger world, multitudes are fed from scanty resources; "results" follow upon our efforts in apparently miraculous fashion. In general, God now bestows His tangible gifts upon us and through us, to the extent that we wonder why everybody hasn't discovered the simple secret of real living, and quite probably we set out to tell them all about it.

3.—"He breaks." Astonished and reassured by the miracles in life, we then snuggle more deeply into God's hands, whereupon, as it were by virtue of His

firmer grip upon us, He begins a loving, dread, and bitterly painful transaction—
"He breaks." This is the famous Passive Dark Night of the Senses and the
even darker Passive Night of the Spirit, about which so many of the classical
authorities wrote. St. John of the Cross gave the "Dark Night" names to the
experience, and in the same area the more modern depth psychology sheds
great light. (Our moment in eternity surely should produce one of those real
masterpieces, those mountain-peak landmarks, which come along every few
hundred years—in this instance written by a genius with equally expert
psychological and spiritual knowledge. Insights into their common subject, the
human soul, gained from these two angles of vision are crying aloud to be
combined.)

"He breaks." To give the experience quick surface treatment: because the
rending must be done on living flesh and tenderized spirit, we writhe most
understandably through these dark nights on our procrustean beds. They are
fierce and gasping times during which God is at the depths, and the self is
both being emptied out and falling into place. Slimy things are welling up out
of the Freudian mists, are being seen in all their horror, are being recognized
as part of one's self, are being reluctantly accepted, and finally are being loved—
"love thine enemy," especially when one is yourself. Of course we resist God
mightily while the vivisection is going on, while all is being taken away, and
we try to cling to life, to faith, and hope with teeth and toenails. Probably most
of us stop Him short of the glory that He really has in mind. Some turn away
and company with Him no more.

4.—"He gave." Those who endure until the true self emerges finally radiate
around themselves something of the real glory of the now indwelling God who
is fashioning them in His own image. What we have here is sanctity, whole-
ness, perfected humanity, because it is intimately united with God. It is full
of grace and hence full of power. Unflinchingly, we have held the 'water' of
self close to the 'flame' of God until He has turned us into 'steam.'

Here we are at grips with one of the most important truths in the world,
diametrically opposed to the naturalistic, the this-worldly, even the Marxist
line that you should endeavor to change man's conditions, for that will change
man. The Christian assertion puts the cart and the horse in the correct
relationship; change man and that will change conditions. Develop by every
possible technique—physical, mental, spiritual—an alert, sensitive, highly
conscious, disciplined, dedicated, creative human spirit that is intimately united
with God, and then observable things begin to happen in the world.

From the pragmatic point of view alone, this is the urgency behind the
living of the spiritual life to the full. The truly religious person does not, can
not, remain in his ivory tower or on his knees in a dim church lighting a candle
and sighing the while. God is not merely very much alive, He is Life itself,

and therefore union with Him brings life. It brings eternal life, which essentially is not a matter of duration but of quality. Through the kind of person produced in the spiritual life "God gives" to His world in the measure made possible by the fullness of the response.

The "giving" is now immeasurably greater than, and of quite different quality from, the blessings He bestowed earlier (in Step 2). Now the really basic hungers of the multitudes are satisfied, with fragments remaining over and above for generations yet unborn. These truly perfected people, these Spirit-filled people, are always the creative and determinative ones in human history. They are Promethean, the real trailblazers of our race. In their measure they are like Jesus. Filled with vision and power themselves, they transmit that enduring power to the world, turning it upside down or right side up. Their contemporaries are not usually kind to them (after all, they're strange; they are not so much contemporary as eternal), but history is in their hands. In every field they build enduringly. Reality enters this world through them.

So important, yet so easily and often overlooked, is this whole paradoxical matter of Christianity's mighty influence upon the world through essential other-worldliness that we shall return to the subject again and again in these pages.

"He took, He blessed, He brake, He gave"—along this course our developing spiritual lives will go as we progress through Purgation to Illumination and then through Mystic Death toward Union. It will be useful now to single out and underline an important fact implicit in both of the analyses sketched.

Spiritual development begins with an "Active" phase, exactly as every kind of growth does. In the Purgative Way and even into the Illuminative stage, we work hard at our own creation and in society around us, employing many disciplines and activities. We obey a Rule of Life, replete with vocal prayers, meditations, self-examinations, fastings, worshipings, sacraments. We go abroad with great energy, rising early and resting late. "When thou wast young, thou girdest thyself, and walkedst whither thou wouldst" describes the phase well, as perhaps it was intended to.

The Purgative Way, in short, is not strictly supernatural. It can with some truth be described as a combination of ethical culture and genuine spirituality, in which both God and man "take arms against a sea of troubles, and by opposing end them." More truly, in it we actively help God toward our own sanctification and that of the world around us in a manner we never will nor can, nor would wish to, later on.

This appears to be as high a level as most of us reach in our earthly lives, and it is a very good level indeed. For that matter, because our perfection is as much a gift from above as it is an accomplishment from below, all we can do "by might" is prepare a sensitive receiving apparatus and then wait for the inrush of Spirit.

"Ascetical Theology" is the technical name given to the branch of truth that concerns itself with the techniques and spiritual gymnastics of the "Active" stage. It is the science of that devotional art. By way of illustration, this book is essentially an essay in the ascetical field for it is chiefly concerned with spiritual rudiments and building blocks. I trust it does not give the impression that we can successfully, by building from the bottom, erect a tower reaching to the sky. On the other hand I most fervently hope it does stress that we must toil upward until we stand atop a sturdy and fairly tall structure, accustomed to a certain giddiness, before God can dare whisk us to the seventh heaven. Spiritual skyscrapers, like physical ones, can only be erected through the application of blueprints, material, and great labor. The study, and especially the application, of Ascetics is really most welcome to God.

It is even welcome to Him if we undertake our work for the second-rate reason that we want to be full of grace. Graceful people are God's supreme desire. To produce them He flings out the universe with lavish hand, grieves over the parts of it that go astray, and labors mightily to bring wanderers back into their designed orbits. This end is sure if, in cooperation with the Divine effort, we give our wills to the working out of our own salvation.

Our cooperative response begins and continues, we repeat, with our diligent efforts—with activity. However, "passivity" (which can and must be carefully distinguished from "quietism") will follow inevitably upon it, if true growth goes forward. At a certain "breaking point," "another shall gird thee, and carry thee whither thou wouldst not."

Our part here, where God's creativity takes over almost entirely, is the activity of stretching forth our arms and willingly accepting what is sent. At this stage one is called upon to 'will God's will,' to abandon one's self to God in the present circumstance, in the utmost reality and with no nonsense about it. In everyone's immortal career there comes the time when "a stronger than he overcometh him and taketh from him all his armour wherein he trusted." To mix metaphors—when one is prepared, and if one is willing, God squeezes him forth, somewhat like toothpaste through a narrow opening, creating a divine image and likeness from the unformed mass that lies back there in the tube. If this does not happen in the present world—and apparently with most of us it does not—it surely will in the next one.

The "passivity" part of the spiritual life is the province of "Mystical Theology," which is introduced here and elsewhere in this book despite the fact that we Actives court grave dangers when we dabble in matters beyond our experience and vocation. My excuse for mentioning the subject is that I fail to see how we can intelligently run the race that is set before us if we do not have at least a dim and far-off glimpse of the ultimate hurdles.

Before we mention a third, and for our purposes the final master pattern of our religious development, we must remind ourselves of the fundamental Christian truth that, in the Incarnation, God and man were joined together again after their separation "in Adam and Eve." Christianity is completely meaningless unless it is realized that in the person of Jesus the reunion of God and man was achieved. It is equally important to know that this was accomplished, not by God lowering Himself to mankind, but by humanity being taken up into God. The spiritual life simply cannot be understood apart from that basic truth.

The importance of the matter compels some elaboration here, beginning with the truth that we are not simply individuals but members of humanity. For good and for ill we are all in one common human nature together. I may wish that I had been born in another galaxy, the farther away the better—and that I lived there at this moment—when that dreadful person down the street flaunts an insufferable self before God and man, but the fact remains that I was born on earth and that his blood will flow nicely in my own veins. When I see our common humanity brutalized and brutalizing by terrorists I may want no part of the outrage, but I am in it, and I am outraged and outrageous in it, nonetheless. Sitting miles away watching it on television, I am torn down in the event.

On the other hand, when in our common human nature Milton writes a poem, Shakespeare a play, Mozart a symphony, we are all thereby ennobled. When Lister, Pasteur, and Salk make medical breakthroughs, we all benefit. Our corporate hearts stop beating while John Glenn blasts off into space; we hold our breath when Neil Armstrong steps onto the moon, because these people carry human nature beyond previous limits, and we know that in our own bones. Armstrong, as he said, did not stand in the moondust alone. All mankind stood there, lifted to new heights, even before another member of our common humanity took the giant step and joined him. Christ did exactly the same, only He carried us higher. In Him, our humanity was taken up into God.

I repeat that the humanity of Jesus is the only humanity there is. It is all the humanity that ever was or ever will be. It is mine at this moment, for example. This nature—not its particular wearer—that is sitting here before a typewriter groping for words has *been* The Word, has perfectly loved, expressed, and served God. In it, Jesus loved, expressed, and served God perfectly for me, and for you, and for all. In our common humanity He presented the whole human race to its creator, making in that presentation a right use of our nature that avails for all of us as we wear it.

An important by-product of this truth that each of us is one with the human race, one with humanity united to God in Christ, is that we cannot make the smallest advance in sanctity without involving others. We cannot take a step closer to human perfection without also carrying the whole human race closer to its ideal.

Herein is sufficient reason and urgency for any individual's entering as deeply as possible into Christ's atonement and thus filling up on behalf of the whole world that which is yet lacking in the taking of humanity into God. We who are in Christ's humanity—the only humanity there is, and which must become totally God-permeated—have in the spiritual life the unique opportunity to pick up the whole world and carry it a bit further. It is heartening to know this, because ultimately one grows weary of what seems like self-improvement. Indeed we often despair of the enormous work and struggle in the spiritual life, especially if it is viewed only as being the effort required to kill off the Old Man in *us*. Often we realize that we don't matter that much.

Perseverance resurges when it is clearly seen that the effort extends beyond our mere selves. We can and will keep at our prayers and disciplines when we see their real point: that our prayers this morning made some difference in Africa, that our abstinence on Friday will reach out to the Middle East, that our almsgiving—this is fairly easy to see—extends to the end of the world.

Thus we come at last to our final master plan of religious growth. It can be stated quite briefly: the individual spiritual life progresses in conformity with the ongoing human life of Christ. In our measure, in our own person, we pass through the stages and events—the "Mysteries"—in the earthly career of Jesus (of man reunited with God). To state this more truly, they pass through us. Mystically considered it could not be otherwise, because the Christian life is essentially the life of Christ relived in each of his members.

Ascetically considered, we have here the real reason why the Church Militant leads us annually through the Christian Year, in which we do not so much remember as relive with personal identification all the events of the Sacred Life, one after the other. It is why the Christian Cultus—Christianity's way of worship and way of life—is indispensable in producing in us the life of Christ. It is why we must (as we shall see) meditate so diligently upon the Sacred Humanity and all the Mysteries. The steady progress of Christ's life is the story of our own lives. He lives and grows in us, and we assist the process in every possible way—sacramentally, intellectually, emotionally, volitionally, morally, dynamically.

To return very briefly to the mystical side of the matter, as everyone knows "we are baptized into the death of God's Son, are buried with Him, and pass with Him through the gates of death to our joyful resurrection." This basic fact involves the truths that along the way we increase with Him in wisdom and stature. We fast and are tempted in the wilderness. We come to the Garden of Gethsemane, we are desolated on the cross, we descend into hell, and all the rest. In short, the Apostles' Creed is true on every level. Not least of these levels is the accuracy of its second paragraph as a description of the spiritual life.

Devotionally this is marvelous beyond words, for to say that wherever He is, I am, is to say also that wherever I am, He is.

Chapter Three

Detachment

STILL ANOTHER general view of the spiritual life, gained from a different approach than that of the previous chapter, shows it to be characterized by, or composed of, the two great elements our Lord called "prayer and fasting." Many other classic names have been given to the basic two-sidedness, the positive and negative bipolarity, of the spiritual life. Familiar pairings are such expressions as "detachment and attachment," "mortification and aspiration," "discipline and desire," "death and resurrection." As the mystics often put it, we must come out of Egyptian bondage in order to enter into the Promised Land.

In familiar statements like, "If any man will come after Me, let him deny himself . . . and follow Me," Christ invariably spoke of the spiritual journey as undertaken with light or even empty knapsack. Classical spirituality, faithful to our Lord, likewise knows nothing of religion that tries to rise on the wings of prayer alone, in the forlorn hope that one is not really chained to the rocks below. All trustworthy guides agree that there are indeed two essentials in the spiritual life. Augustine Baker, for example, based the entire teaching of his massive *Holy Wisdom* on the twin pillars of mortification and prayer, which support the whole spiritual edifice. Of them he writes, "Mortification without prayer will be but superficial, or, it is to be feared, hypocritical; and prayer with a neglect of mortification will be heartless, distracted, and of small value."

Of these two matters, prayer and fasting, we discuss the latter first because of the strong suspicion that of the two inseparable equals, fasting—disentanglement from this world—is more equal than prayer—aspiration toward the other one. There is indeed a whole "negative" school that affirms this. St. John of the Cross is an outstanding spokesman for the group: "Would that I could convince spiritual persons that the road to God consists . . . in one necessary thing only, in knowing how to deny themselves in earnest, inwardly and outwardly . . . and if he be deficient in this exercise, which is the sum and root of all virtue, all he may do will be but beating the air . . . utterly profitless, notwithstanding great meditations."

Before we dismiss Saint John's opinion as a hopeless medievalism, we would do well to pause and consider that the greatest spiritual directors of every era have also been more concerned to know how their disciples stand in such matters as penitence, humility, discipline, obedience, detachment, poverty, simplicity, mortification, and the like than what they are doing in their prayer lives. They think that "fasting" gives the better indication of where we truly are. They feel that we have to pour out the dirty water before the bottle can be filled with clean. They are sure we are rich in proportion to the number of things we can do without. They are convinced that the degree of death determines the amount of life. They know we are free when it really does not matter to us whether we abound, or are in want.

In this they are not inventing a new religion, but are being quite faithful to the greatest of all spiritual directors. Jesus knew that self is the only thing that stands between us and God. He knew that self, which fearfully builds all kinds of protective barriers around its tenderness, must be lovingly deprived of all these prison walls before it can step out and stand free—be deprived of them first by our own efforts and then by accepting as gracefully as possible the mighty actions of God to this end. He knew, in short, that the significant story of our lives is the tale of the purification of our faith in God, until at last this trust becomes sheer, needing no support and even no reward. And so He said a multitude of things like "Sell all and follow Me, . . . he that loseth his life for My sake shall find it, . . . no man can serve two masters, . . . a rich man shall hardly enter into the kingdom of heaven, . . . every one that hath forsaken shall receive, . . . blessed are ye poor." His own earthly life, from manger to cross, suited action perfectly to words.

Disquietingly familiar as all this is to us, we nevertheless recoil from it. Something within us whispers, and everything around us shouts, loudly enough to overcome the disquieting witness of a thousand vital Thoreaus that God could not possibly expect us to forsake earth in order to enter heaven. The inner voice bids us listen well to that chorus from our world-affirming era, evermore chanting its siren song that only insanity renounces this world in the hope of finding abundant life.

On a deeper level, we sense the sharp contrast between the "success patterns" of the two conflicting worlds; in the supernatural one, the Kingdom of God, we are dealing essentially with what is *given*—with what is given us, and what we give. The child of God is seen to be a dependent, to be quite literally a child who lives by grace and in grace—and grace is a given. So the basic supernatural virtue, or attitude, is the ability to receive. "Open thy mouth wide and I will fill it." The spiritual life is one of letting God come in and flow through.

On the other hand, in the natural world we make progress, we adapt successfully, we survive and arrive by being actively on the attack. We batter hard and continuously against the stern reality around us, and if we don't make it yield to us we at least have the satisfaction of going down fighting. The stress is heavily upon the activity—even the assertion—of self. "Thrust yourself forward persistently, and thus fulfill yourself," they say. "Get power. And after you've gotten it, hold on to it tightly."

Thus stretched and torn between two worlds, in our practice of religion we do not really journey from the one toward the other. Typically, like the Israelites at the beginning of their Exodus, we wander rather aimlessly in a wasteland between two countries. Often we look back toward the remembered fleshpots of Egypt, only to find no great joy there any more. Yet when we face about again, the Promised Land is a misty mirage that continually eludes us. Most of us spend all of our unhappy lives in this neither-neither land, forever attempting our compromise between two worlds. We never really accept the truth—that we must come all the way out of the one before we can enter into the other, and that then, amazingly, we actually have them both.

In sober truth, nothing but personal trial will convince us that Christ knew what He was talking about when He said we cannot serve both God and Mammon. Until we actually try it, we shall never really know that in order to hold to the one we must despise the other. However, it may encourage us toward taking a real plunge to have it pointed out again that the human soul is spirit, pure energy, and therefore must always be "doing something" and tending somewhere. Stretched as it is between two forces, it will inevitably fall back into and be swallowed by mere Nature, if its activity is not consistently directed out of Nature. One of its two great attractions must atrophy from disuse, while the other gains strength from exercise.

Another general reminder may also be useful. Somewhere along the line we all learned the truth—startling when it first dawned upon us—that our desires are not a fixed quantity. Earthly desire, for example, is almost infinitely flexible in both directions. To the great joy of manufacturers and pitchmen, today's luxury smoothly becomes tomorrow's necessity. The converse of this is just as true, but the advertising fraternity sleeps soundly of nights because "strait is the gate, and narrow is the way, which leadeth unto life, and few there be that find it." Unfortunately, those who are indeed available to testify that the narrow way does lead to richer life make no great noise about it. If asked, however, they will happily certify to this and to a more important matter also— that a taste of God increases our taste for God, without possibility of satiety.

However, only personal mortification will actually enroll us among these happy few, demonstrating to us in a living process of daily dying the truth about "real life," that consummation we are all seeking and which the spiritual life faithfully promises to bring. This truth begins with, or rests solidly upon, the healthy premise that the world of nature is neither hostile to nor destructive of created beings, even of us human beings who are part clay and part spirit. On the contrary, all things in this sacramental world were means of grace to us, by original divine intention. Potentially they still are. The difficulty is that they are only so to a person who does not seek them as ends in themselves— to a soul that also conforms to the original divine intention and is "full of grace." Unfortunately, that phrase describes none of us now, since the Fall of Man cost us our integrity.

Universal experience testifies that very few things speak of God—and then neither loudly nor often—to the person who is enmeshed in those things. Usually a loaf of bread is merely a loaf of bread, period. On occasion a mountain, or a grassy glade, or a meal with friends, or a quiet evening by the fire may transmit something of God. However, only individual experience can choose the really relevant illustrations here, and that is exactly the point; in the beginning only a few items, different according to individual responsiveness, are windows that let God in. The rest are walls that bar Him out. Early in our development, in fact, we are apt to become impatient with "spiritual people," or with poets, who allege that they find God in every rosebush, including its thorns. We feel they are dupes or posers.

Yet the poets are right. We are indeed seeing all the truth of reality only when we are seeing fact and meaning at the same time. All really mature thinking is at least parabolic, two-leveled; a mind completely in touch with the nature of the universe perforce moves on *four* levels at once. On the way to this end, as spirituality develops, more and more things begin to become means of grace, avenues of God, food for the soul. Ultimately we are truly at one with Nature, which we then find fully restored to its original intended order as a sacramental whole for us. In this consummation nothing—no event, no feeling, no temptation, no work, no suffering, no blade of grass—is spiritually meaningless. As we then pass through things temporal, we lose not the things eternal.

The verifiable thesis of Christian asceticism is, in short, that only the other-worldly person can really enjoy life and all the things of life—a tremendous and a true paradox. Only the spiritual person is free among things, not enslaved by them. Christ came, indeed, in order that we might have life thus more abundantly, not less so.

He came to set right the human situation so beautifully expressed by the geniuses who wrote Genesis. In the beginning, we repeat in their terms, "God saw everything that He had made, and behold, it was very good." The man and the woman then shared this same point of view as they lived to the full in nature, naked and yet unashamed, because their clear and unselfconscious sight penetrated unhindered through the surface to the truths beneath. After they fell from grace, Genesis ironically notes that "their eyes were opened," and they had to make clothes because their gaze stopped at the surface of things. They became so self-conscious that they were conscious of little else, which is practically the definition of human sickness.

This blind surface vision is the condition of all of us children of Adam and Eve, who begin our eternal journey far down on the bodily level, in touch with reality on its dull surface level but deaf to sermons in stones and tongues in trees. Intellectual development does bring overtone and insight, sufficiently satisfying so that many are content to stunt their growth at that point. In truth they are not far from the Kingdom of God, although they are not yet free on earth. They are only living in a larger cage with wider apertures between the bars, for Mind is not Spirit or Self but only a high 'faculty' thereof. In example, knowledge has little to do with the acquiring of moral virtues. The indispensable tool, self-denial—which may begin with childhood's fasting from candy in Lent, and which ends in maturity when One stronger than we are finally detaches us from the last of our attachments—is necessary if we are to break out into complete human freedom both here and hereafter.

By means of denying things to our selves we learn the art of indirection— that we cannot look straight at things, as it were, and have them whole; we only see them in right perspective when we look at them out of the corners of our eyes. More importantly, we succeed in denying our selves to things, thus preserving them for more proper worship. On the final level, in which we begin to deny self itself, God comes swiftly to our aid and in awesome ways helps us push our selves aside. We then begin to glimpse Him at the center where He always is, but where we heretofore have failed to see Him.

Now discerning Him there with considerable clarity because our gaze is less attracted to side issues and more concentrated on Him, we begin to reclaim the basic quality that Adam and Eve tossed away for us all. When the "creaturely sense" is fully ours again, and when self is completely laid aside, we step freely back into the Garden of Eden. We have successfully used St. John of the Cross's ascetic means—"To have pleasure in everything, seek pleasure in nothing"— and have arrived at St. Paul's glorious consummation, "As having nothing, and yet possessing all things." We have followed our Lord through the grave and with Him have risen to newness of life.

In brief, St. Augustine expresses the basic human problem by saying truly, "The things of the world are for our use, not for our enjoyment. That which is for our enjoyment is the Father, the Son, and the Holy Ghost." And Francis Thompson gives the solution, when he speaks of self-denial in the only really proper way:

> "All which I took from thee I did but take,
>   Not for thy harms,
>
> But just that thou might'st seek it in My arms.
>   All which thy child's mistake
>
> Fancies as lost, I have stored for thee at home:
>   Rise, clasp My hand, and come."

Chapter Four

Discipline

SURELY MANY PEOPLE reach the level of grace and freedom described at the close of the previous chapter. Mortification has quite accomplished its preliminary work by breaking the hold of earth upon them and then restoring it to them. In close union with the Bridegroom here and now, completely detached from all lesser attractions, they have no need to concentrate any longer on particular "external" denials. Set free in the world by their holy indifference to it, they can direct their continuing mortifications against interior matters like their hopes and fears. A few of these adventurers pass through the farthest reaches of the Mystic Death, ultimately emerging from the Night of the Spirit to stand tiptoe on the very mountain top.

Christian ascetics points us all toward this goal. It holds out to us the glorious liberty of the sons of God, in which we cry 'Abba, Father,' but it also enables the destined end by providing the necessary means. It does not, as it were, throw us into the World Series before practice has made us ready to play in that arena. Until we sandlotters achieve such stature, we can well forget the "mystical" analysis of fasting given in the former chapter and devote ourselves to its ascetic practice. Down on this level we deal with the fundamentals that begin to cut us loose from the clutch of the "flesh, the world, and the devil."

"The flesh, the world, the devil"—thus classical terminology pinpoints the only three sources of all our innumerable temptations. The familiar phrase clarifies (even simplifies, without immediately making easier) the lifelong battle against sin. Its exposure of temptation's only three roots does, however, direct our main campaign against the enemies' supply lines. We see that our essential warfare is as much ascetic as it is moral—that it deals with root causes as well as with daily effects. We realize that as we cut roots the unsavory fruit on the branches will begin to wither. In our better moments we even know that we battle our enemies, root and branch, "in the name of the Lord of hosts." Long ago our Lord won victory for us on the same triple front. It 'only' remains that His victory for us becomes His victory in us.

'The flesh' brings into view our animal inheritance. A more modern but less capable word might be 'Body'—that earthy part of our composite spirit-in-body nature.

Ideally, Body is Spirit's servant rather than its master. Ideally, it serves Spirit in perfect obedience and perfectly expresses Spirit as a supple instrument. It is an agile, responsive part of one indivisible whole.

Needless to say, in lifelong practical experience, that is not the way we have come to know the interrelationship of Spirit and Body. Our parents handed down to us an awkward situation. Making our bodies gracefully responsive to our wills calls for strenuous discipline—limiting that word now to mean the beginning way in which we bring Body into subjection. On this lovely afternoon in early fall I paused at our high school's athletic field to watch the boys practicing—individually, corporately, and painstakingly acquiring their skills. As I drove on past the Country Club, I saw another kind of discipline going on, as golfers interminably hit their shots off the practice tee seeking to bring Body under the sway of Spirit. At this moment, in two houses within my hearing, children are practicing scales or something. One of them is doing it on the piano, but the other, all too clearly, aspires to be a trumpeter. I pray that they both will speedily acquire freedom through their discipline. I realize that I myself am not free to play the piano—let alone the trumpet—because I abandoned the effort at an early age. On the other hand, I rejoice that I can typewrite more than adequately, because I maintained that discipline. My fingers do what I want them to, even without my telling them about it. My problems in writing are not in the mechanical line.

So it is in any field of excellence. Between willing and doing there is a great gulf fixed, even on this beginning level. It is bridged by discipline, continued until Body expresses Spirit; until one is free, on this level.

Flesh, or Body, also has its more dynamic surges. Those good things called sex, or hunger, or thirst, have a built-in twist that tends toward their inordinate indulgence—with the wrong people, at the wrong time, in the wrong degree—and hence to their being spoiled in lust, gluttony, drunkenness. When dealing with Body on this level we have to go beyond mere discipline. Here we enter the field of self-denial. Here we have not merely to say "no," but to effect that "no" by means of determined ascetic practices—by "the custody of the eyes," "the avoidance of occasions of sin," and a hundred others—if we are to be free from enslavement. Real selfhood on the higher levels, with the will ruling our whims and emotions rather than subject to them, is otherwise impossible.

The proper time has now come for spelling out, explicitly, that the "self-made man" is not being extolled herein. As we are all aware, if only from rueful introspection, self-manufacture slides all too readily from self-satisfaction into self-righteousness and then to the exaltation of self upon the seat of the scornful. From that vantage point, which looks down upon the common herd, one can begin to despise and ultimately to hate those weak-willed drifters engaged in messing up their own and others' lives. Under certain conditions, the next step is to cleanse the world of them by means of firing squad or gas chamber. More lenient autocrats, also unmindful of "let both grow together until the harvest," do sometimes content themselves with mere exile of the recalcitrants, extending hope of restoration to decent society should the banished sinners straighten up and live blamelessly for twenty years.

However, censoriousness in any degree cannot result from proper understanding of the spiritual life. True Christian ascetics always springs from thankful awareness that God entered the world not because of the righteous but in order to seek and to save sinners, beginning with me. It fully rejoices in the heart, fact, and miracle of the Gospel—that God "loves us first and improves us later," not the other way around. What sustains it is the triumphant truth that God loves saint and sinner perfectly, just the way they both are at the moment. He will never love either of them more than he does "right now," at the pinnacle of their virtue or in the depths of their sins. He loves them both fully, all of the time.

Christian ascetics, the science of sanctification, moves forward from this firm base to consider how we cooperate with God in producing in us what we are not yet, but what He does have in view for us. Hence, what is being written here about discipline is in the context of that process of becoming. It is a discussion for those who really love God, His "standards," His being, and who want so desperately to be more like Him that they ache to spurn downward beneath their feet all those things within themselves that drag them from Him, the while they aspire eagerly to have His nature really take root in them.

In short, Christian ascetics remains faithful to our Lord Himself, the very Love of God who came searching in this world, and who said to those He found such things as "If thine eye, or thine hand, offend thee and cause thee to stumble—pluck it out, cut it off. It is profitable for thee that one of thy members should perish, and not that thy whole body should be cast into hell." This can easily be said in a loving, even a pleading, tone of voice and surely was.

'The world' is an even more subtle, more powerful, and more pervading enemy of the soul than is 'the flesh.' In surface illustration of its external standards we can cite such apparent trivialities as "The Joneses," or "The country club set," or "What 'they' say." 'They' say things like "Get status. Get rich. Know the right people, go to the right places, wear the right clothes, say the right things, drive the right car."

Even with these illustrations it is apparent what 'the world' means—false standards, which readily seduce our pursuing desires into inordinate ambition to attain them. It is also apparent that 'the world's' pressure is always all around us and finds ready response within us. In fact we always more than half believe 'the world' until we become totally detached from it, as we have seen. For that matter, the Church Militant—except during rare brief epochs of reform—herself goes a great distance arm in arm with 'the world.' It may be somewhat consoling to recall that the Apostolic Band itself did also, up to the very end. Even at the Last Supper the Apostles entered into one more argument about who was the greatest among them. And there once again our broken-hearted but ever-patient Lord gave them further example and instruction on true standards, as He had a score of times before.

The illustration is introduced not to document Apostolic Succession in the modern Church but to underline our problem. The world is tangibly all about us, bearing in on us with vast power—and it is almost precisely opposed to the standards of Christ. As we have already indicated, it is at the antipodes from Mangers, from a poverty-stricken upbringing in tiny forgotten Nazareth, from a mature life spent without money or success, and without even a final grave of His own. Hence there is a truly fierce battle on this ground as we attempt to move, and be drawn, from one world to the other. Herein is sufficient reason, unaided by the many others, why the spiritual person has hard going in this world. All powers outside him, and more than half of those within him, are directed against him when he decides to pitch his camp elsewhere. Unavoidably, he often doubts the wisdom of his choice, which seeks security in the invisibles and intangibles. Often he doubts our Lord's wisdom on the matter. Again and again he ponders Christ's words, so consonant with his life, on the subject: "You cannot serve God and Mammon. It is impossible. I grant you that all around you they plunge for Mammon, in anxiety about what they shall eat, what they shall drink, what they shall wear, and how they can send the children to college. But I say unto you. . . ." Often he falters, often he thinks God has either forgotten him or simply cannot deliver the goods, often he starts back across the street to rejoin former companions who are making steady progress in the world and leaving him far behind—with his wife and children bearing the brunt. Then once again he hesitates, because an inner voice is whispering something about integrity.

This is sufficient anguish for any man. However, if he persists in a course of discipline against the world—persists in the cultivation of simplicity, in detachment from created things, in the avoidance of the occasions of sin, in the daily carrying of his own particular cross, in the discipline of his desires, in the constant submitting of his own dear judgments to the bar of Christ—he will come to the time when he simply cannot recross that street. He cannot return to the world, because his years of refusing it have put it from him beyond recall—and yet he has little to show for those years. The world is gone, but there is nothing to put in its place.

He has now come to one of life's most excruciating situations. He is struggling fiercely for a sense of God's care in all circumstances; struggling to make real to himself that he is indeed, despite the lack of evidence, in God's loving hands. In St. Bernard's famous terms, he is passing from "The Love of God for Self" to "The Love of God for God," and he finds himself standing in Job's company, trying to pray, "Though He slay me, yet will I put my trust in Him." Prayer is almost the only solace and strength he knows, and now even prayer seems to fail. It is of no apparent avail in this searching passage.

Naturally his shivering and naked soul should, and undoubtedly will, keep on gasping its sometimes hopeful, sometimes despairing, sometimes even bitter cries. These cries will soon be answered, but in a strange way. The fact is that the reliable tool of detachment has done its work. Its persevering use in spurning spurious securities has broken refuge after refuge. Prayer at this time often begs that one may be taken back into those former havens, but this is impossible because they don't exist any more. The only possible direction is forward—across the bridge between the Active and the Passive spiritual life. In answering the prayers, God will act on the prepared soul and give it even more deprivations until, as we have said before, faith becomes sheer. Then at last the clouds roll back.

This fearsome passage waits for all who begin and continue a course of opposition to the world, but it waits in love, for only thus can the problem of the Double Will be solved. However, on this course it is solved, and we do thus come to genuine selfhood, to "The Love of self for God," with its stability, security, sure purpose, freedom from fear, and all the other precious fruits of living confidence in the living God. We then know that just to be God's is sufficient for all things.

No one has ever gone to the heights of this resurrection without passing completely through the death toward which fasting leads, and which it makes possible, but even this is not the most important matter. What is really important is that the world needs precisely those who are not conformed to it, enslaved by it, fearful in it, if *it* is to be led to the heights. The point is so vital that we pause here to recapitulate swiftly what has so far been said about "fasting" and to add some observations not yet made, illustrating all of them by the requirements of The Book of Common Prayer in this area. The somewhat circuitous route will bring us back to the point just left dangling.

We began our discussion by stressing the necessity of discipline, for example, in helping to produce self-control. We observed that this is quite in line with universal commonsense experience; for instance, with the truism that parents who deny their children self-denial are, in their unkind solicitude, closing the door to growth and glory and condemning their offspring to self-indulgent mediocrity among the beasts that perish. We indicated that saying "no" on occasion in little matters does train an individual's will, preparing him somewhat for that rare and basic virtue, Obedience. It is a small beginning step away from the prison of "My will be done" toward the freedom of "Thy will be done." Between these only two ultimate aspirations of any human being there is a great gulf fixed, which we cannot begin to span unless we systematically deny some harmless things to ourselves—jam on our bread during the forty weekdays of Lent, to take a tired example.

The Friday abstinence also operates in its small way on this level and opens the door to the consideration of new aspects of ascetical fasting, the first of which is the close association of self-denial and recollection. Friday's abstinence continually calls to mind the Lord's complete self-giving on that day, just as Sunday's festival recalls His resurrection, and we do need the one reminder as much as the other. Indeed, we need the repeated assurance that the two are inseparably connected; that there can be no Easter without Good Friday, either in our Lord's life or in our own.

In this same context of recollection, it is a fact of experience that the Lenten obligation of special self-denial—no tobacco, say—does keep a person everlastingly reminded of positive items in his Rule, for example that this Lent in the help of God he will learn to hold his tongue somewhat. Ash Wednesday's complete fast, at the start of this endeavor, deeply impresses the resolution. Good Friday's equally total fast, at the end of the struggle, consummates it all by bringing strongly to mind the Good Friday fact. For this "recollective" reason alone, the Church wisely requires a "measure of abstinence" that does enable growth in devotion and virtue. Without the constant daily reminder of a chosen abstinence, we are all too prone to forget about our 'spiritual' and rather vague aspirations.

Furthermore, the accepted abstinence acts as an all-important indication that the spiritual life is lived in space and time, in a physical body, here and now. A constant temptation besets us to be "purely spiritual"—to practice religion possibly appropriate to angels but definitely not to men and women. We readily forget that a human being is a Body-Spirit complex, not a pure spirit. Words do not impress this fact upon us with anything like the power that feast-and-fast has. It is simply not sufficient, not complete, that human beings commune with God only with their minds. We must both toast him in wine and adore him with hunger. The Son of Man "came eating and drinking," to the extent that He was dubbed "a gluttonous man and a winebibber," and He also "fasted forty days and forty nights." To neglect either of these elements is to cut ourselves off from the human race, throughout whose history both feasting and fasting have been universal phenomena, spontaneously springing up in connection with deep realities like love, triumph, joy, homecoming, repentance, mourning, dedication, sacrifice. Human nature craves devotional expression by means of body, mind, and soul.

Unfortunate religious heritage has tended to obscure, in our time, a further aspect of fasting. For some centuries now, individualism and subjectivism have been rampant in religion, with melancholy results upon true spirituality.

Wholesome religion pays these elements scant attention. It rightly cares very little how I "feel" and astonishingly little about "I." The Book of Common Prayer, for example, continues the group life of the Apostolic Band. Faithful to its title, it expresses and conveys a corporate spirituality—common worship, common doctrine, common lifestyle, and discipline in common. Corporate religion is, obviously, the only kind appropriate to the Body of Christ.

Since we will be examining other facets of this truth later on, here we confine ourselves to noting that the members of this Body sit down at one training table. From it, no individual merely picks and chooses in accordance with his own tastes and feelings, as from a smorgasbord, but takes some of everything the corporate diet provides for the well-being of the entire Body. In short, fasts as well as festivals are measures, marks and means of spiritual allegiance and obedience to our common Lord, to His Church, and—we are now rapidly approaching our delayed point—to His world. Through them we suit our actions to our aspirations. As with our lips we daily profess allegiance to the Church, so with our fasts we actually allow the Church to enter our "private" lives in such an intimate way as intruding upon our dining room tables. Could there be a better way to remind ourselves that eating forbidden fruit neither produces the larger freedoms, nor serves to create union among people (they say that Adam and Eve, having broken their fast, immediately began to argue), nor deepens loyalty to God our Father and to Holy Mother Church? Our fragmented modern world, descended from the said Adam and Eve, desperately needs such a strongly bound together corporate religion.

The mystics, firmly based in this corporal and corporate awareness, soar upward from it to tell us that no man is an individual entity in regard to fasting, just as he is no monad in other regards. The Church, while not wholly given over to mysticism, nevertheless seemed to be implying the same truth when, for example, she bade us abstain and pray on the Ember Days with intention for her clergy. In so doing she raised the point that vicarious fasting makes sense and brings strength to both faster and fastee. However that may be, even as there are times—of bereavement, for example—in our individual lives when Nature calls us to fast ("the thought of food simply nauseates me"), just so on occasions of great danger and potential disaster the Nation challenges us all to a corporate fast. Intuitively at such times we know, and readily respond to, the rightness of this summons to "sanctify a fast, call a solemn assembly." At those fraught times the whole tone of our corporate life sounds a clearer note, an octave higher than prevails in more ordinary days. Furthermore, on these bound together occasions the dedicated group measureably makes more impact on the rest of the world than a like number of individuals would. History records numerous occasions when the whole was greater than the sum of its parts. Times when mutual concern, mutually expressed and conveyed by a dedicated clan both praying and fasting together—wholly devoted in body and soul to God and His purposes—had awesome power to move mountains.

This brings us to the point left hanging. If we combine what has just been said with the whole discussion in the previous chapter, we are again face to face with the paradox of otherworldliness, now on the corporate as well as the individual level. So we assert again, with the Apostolic Church as one witness, that otherworldliness simply does have not only more freedom but much more power in this world than worldliness does. Indeed, we reiterate a constant theme—that the world has little reason to note, nor to remember long, those who are totally immersed in it. True creativity, built upon enduring foundations, always comes from outside this world into it. It comes from those who are held up above the earth, from which vantage point they see it somewhat whole.

Above all in our present context, high consecration and real creativity come into this world through Thoreau's lean men, who are not merely gross animal feeders in the larva state of human development. With the unsluggish bodies that are inseparably linked to alert minds and spirits, they are both keen to perceive the motions of God and to effect these inspirations. They fast with our Lord, to the Father who sees in secret, and through them He rewards His world openly. Thus alerted by daily reminders and ennoblers, these people are more ready than most to hear God's voice. Always somewhat trained and ready in the spirit and practices of Obedience, they are prepared and willing to respond when a call comes. They are in the individual and corporate habit of saying "yes," and they are in the habit of disregarding, or at least deferring, mere personal inclination. God can work through their orderly beings to bring order to other parts of His world.

Freud and his followers have shed great light into the murky depths of the deepest widest area of our continuing spiritual warfare—that third enemy of the soul classically called "the devil." They have shown us that this concept includes all the depths of our evolving animal and racial backgrounds lying below the surface and continually surging to break through. Here, in addition to the personified Malice that stalks about a fallen world, is all the explosive content of the subconscious, and possibly of the unconscious, which wells up seeking to confound us, to horrify us, to destroy us. Here is an apparently endless depth of dynamic, ranging from such surface matters as irritation, ill temper, unreasoning likes and dislikes, laziness, down through envies, fears, guilts, perversions, sadisms, surging hatreds, endlessly on and on. Here is the corrupt and rotten heart of man, incredibly prolific as any Hydra. Jesus knew all about it. "From within, out of the heart of man, proceed evil thoughts, adulteries, murders, thefts, covetousness, blasphemy, pride, foolishness." St. Paul also knew. "For the good that I would I do not; but the evil which I would not, that I do. Now if I do that I would not, it is no more I that do it, but sin that dwelleth in me. . . . O wretched man that I am! Who shall deliver me from the body of this death?" This realization that we are not masters in our own houses has been recognized by every other sensitive human soul throughout all the recorded centuries.

In our own day psychiatry is building solid roads through this swamp, roads demonstrably leading to self-knowledge, self-acceptance, and ultimate freedom. Yet history shows that the spiritual life, faithfully and fully pursued until one enters the Contemplative Way, has been the King's Highway to selfhood, the time-tested way for changing human nature permanently.

Contemplation—that experiential awareness of reality culminating in the pure intuition of God—is the most truly human act. Hence it is a peculiarly dreadful thing that in our society the contemplative powers of man, which have been left unexercized for so long, are seriously atrophied. And it is a peculiarly fine thing that in our day many efforts are being made to unwrap this mummy. The contemplative powers of man *must* be reactivated if man is to become himself—become integrated, achieve selfhood and self-expression—and if his world is to become humanized by becoming God-centered.

The spiritual life looks toward this end. Given opportunity, God has led millions of souls carefully and lovingly along, bringing them ever closer to reality while avoiding blowing them apart by letting them see too much too soon. "I have yet many things to say unto you, but you cannot bear them now" He has said, and he has suited both sides of that action to His word. Given opportunity, He will do the same in us, ultimately penetrating to the core. St. Francis de Sales has some comforting words on this most important aspect of fasting: "Our perfection consists in fighting against our imperfections . . . and it is our privilege in this war that we are certain to vanquish so long as we are willing to fight."

St. Paul says the same, explicitly bringing God into the situation: "He who hath begun a good work in you will perfect it." And Jesus Himself has the supreme, the last word: "Blessed are they which do hunger and thirst after righteousness, for they shall be filled." Our persevering desire for God's Kingdom is, to say the least, matched by God's persevering desire to bestow it: "Fear not . . . it is my father's good pleasure to give you the kingdom." So who can attain? Anyone with the grace of perseverance. Anyone who "endure(s) to the end;" who does not fall down and stay down under the assaults of life. Just anyone who does not commit the fatal sin against the Holy Ghost—the sin of quitting, the sin of despair. Anyone who, however feebly, keeps on asking and seeking and knocking. For abetting that feebleness in our efforts is the power of God, whose purposes fail not.

Ascetically, our fight against "the devil" lies in the general fields of self-examination, penitence, and confession. We have already indicated that this begins, in the Purgative Way, by establishing the nightly habit of taking self-inventory by reviewing the day just past. We have also indicated that this will undoubtedly be done 'in general' and will begin on the surface level with words, deeds, omission, and overt thoughts.

We have also indicated that, in the Illuminative Way, this searching process becomes a fairly thorough and particular seeking down the highways and byways of one especial weakness, a ferreting toward its roots, an investigation of its sources and deep motives, with appropriate action following. Needless to say, part of that appropriate action is the deliberate practice of a virtue opposed to our vice.

Finally we have stated that ultimately, in the Mystic Death, God Himself at our depths begins to bring those depths up. Our preparatory activities— disciplines, self-denials, mortifications, Rule of Life, examinations, and confessions have prepared the soil. When God sees that our voluntary fastings have made us aware that only through the grave and gate of death can we pass to our joyful resurrection, He lovingly thrusts us into a genuine death in life. We move from the predominately Active to the predominately Passive life. We begin to be acted upon. The Passive Nights of Sense and Spirit close about us, and in that bitter deprivation we are purified to the depths of our being. Souls and bodies purified in this ultimate fasting are the channels through which God flows into the world in the abundant way to which we so often allude.

We abandon our discussion of fasting, then, at the point where we are about to begin a consideration of The Sacrament of Reconciliation, the Prayer Book's fine term for sacramental forgiveness. Universal experience testifies that this Sacrament of the Dead is *the* gateway to the truly spiritual life. We will give it the individual treatment that its importance demands.

Chapter Five

Forgiveness

THE HUMAN SOUL, gleefully abetted by the devil and too often by travestied religion, is prone to consider itself a greater sinner than God is a forgiver. Evidence is abundant that most of us limp through our lives hag-ridden and crippled by guilt. So although it has already been urged in these pages that God loves us fully just as we are, it seems wise to consider anew the subject of sin and forgiveness, at some length and with particular application.

"What is God like?" is the most important question in the universe. Among Christians, the answer is "Look at Jesus Christ and see." When we look at Him to see the nature of forgiveness, we note that it is a total atmosphere, a constant attitude, an unchanging state of being that is illustrated by many particular acts of doing. "Father, forgive them. . . ." springs to mind as a good example of a particular act. Some scholars have suggested that the phrase was whispered repeatedly while the crucifying nails were being driven in. Certainly it expresses a forthgiving attitude in our Lord, unconditioned by any receptive apparatus on the part of His tormenters.

Other particular instances of this same unchanging disposition appear throughout the Gospel story, almost wherever we look. For example, magnanimity dominates the Sermon on the Mount, with its extra mile, its cloak as well as coat, its light shining in darkness, its love of enemy, its other cheek. Again, St. Luke's "gospel in the Gospel" gives Christ's lovely triad of tales about the lost sheep, the lost coin, the lost son. Further, we recall the individuals dead in sin, or dead in fact, whom our Lord loosed and let go. For good measure, pressed down and running over, in final illustration we can cite Peter's direct question about forgiveness—"How oft? . . . Seven times?"—and our Lord's response of "seventy times seven", which not even a hopelessly legalistic mind can distort from its true meaning. Lest it should, however, Christ then went on to say that God is like a compassionate king who freely forgave his servant the unthinkable, the unpayable, ten thousand talents.

In brief, our Lord is forgiveness itself; the frequent Gospel illustrations simply witness to what He unchangingly is. He is forthgivingness. In the beginning He was with God, and at the appointed time He came forth to us. Perhaps above all, He came not because we deserved Him but because we needed Him.

Like our Lord who came thence, the Kingdom of God is gracious with mercy and forgiveness, not grim with law and justice. The logic of Divinity reasons, "My beloved children are perishing in sin, therefore I will go forth to them." Hence the fundamental truth about forgiveness is what we stated in a different connection—that God has already extended it completely to us.

The wonder of the Gospel is that God has already forgiven us all that we have been and done, all that we are and do, and all that we shall ever be and will do. He does not measure in measure, does not give *quid pro quo,* does not hold back His forgiveness until we make our confessions. Even our penitence does not, as it were, lay hands on God and wheedle favor out of Him by blandishment. The favor is there all the time.

Some primitive theology—much of which lingers into our era—was not yet aware of this truth and hence made attempts to bargain with God. It imagined a contract relationship between Him and us whereby, if we performed our side of an agreement, God had to fulfill His part. But since our Lord, full of grace and truth, came forth into the world revealing the real nature of our Father-son relationship, we Christians should know better. We should know that we do not, can not, force an attitude of grudging approval, or reluctant forgiveness, or complete acceptance on God's part by anything that we do. The unchanging God is unchangingly loving and forgiving.

In spite of St. Paul, who discerned all this clearly and spent his life trying to communicate it, one of Christianity's central problems has always been to convince the world of this incredible truth about God. It is, in fact, terribly hard to believe. Unrelenting nature does not operate on this level, and hence we do not learn it there. Human society, organized on the basis of law—which makes social life bearable, but nothing more—does not reveal it to us. Our own hearts find it exceedingly hard to forgive and accept ourselves, and we project our own reluctance onto God.

Only life in the spiritual world, the world of grace, can make divine graciousness real to us. However, we repeat that all the vast labor involved in the practice of the disciplined ascetic life must be viewed for what it really is and does. Our active effort does not earn merit, does not acquire salvation, does not lay violent hands upon God and make Him bestow grace. Rather, it digests His 'prevenient' grace—His grace which is "there"—preceding our decision to cooperate with it. It appropriates, makes real to our resisting selves, the eternal facts of life.

Prayer, meditation, study, discipline—these do not create truth nor wring it from a grudging God. They tune us in to the truth that is always there. In more particular example, confession essentially helps us to believe, really to know and savor, the astonishing truth that God loves, forgives, and accepts us just as we are.

Unless we hold all this firmly in mind, the impression will almost surely be created that by careful self-examination, contrition, confession, and amendment of life we alter God's disposition toward us; as it were, change His frown into a smile. It is far closer to the truth that the Sacrament of Reconciliation changes *our* frown into a smile. Fortunately, the Anglican discipline of this sacrament conforms to the point of view sketched in this chapter. That discipline urges us to make our confessions sacramentally when we cannot quiet our consciences, cannot bring ourselves to believe in the forgiveness of sins without this definite pledge to assure us thereof. "A pledge to assure us thereof" is, so often, what so many of us need. Some people need it more than others, for various reasons ranging the whole gamut from dreadful insecurity to the most overweening pride. Hence the kindly Anglican discipline of the Sacrament of Reconciliation is loosely stated as "All may use it, none must, and some should."

It was indicated at the close of the previous chapter that those who use this sacrament are so well satisfied with its importance in their spiritual lives that they universalize on personal experience and proclaim it to be *the* doorway into spiritual reality. The writer cheerfully admits to being of this persuasion and acknowledges the fact to make clear that sin is not being minimized here. Neither is it being said offhandedly, "Well now, we do have the Sacrament of Reconciliation, you know, and perhaps you might like to try it some day."

On the contrary, I am desolated by sin, and I strongly urge every soul to claim sacramental absolution. I encourage all to nerve themselves for that dread first confession—at the end of which a good Confessor will probably say, "Is that all, my son?"—and then to be regular penitents throughout their Purgative Way, in which they are getting rid of the only real obstacle to spiritual growth, themselves. Confession twelve times a year, on or about the first of each month, is not too much for this. Five times a year—on Shrove Tuesday, Easter Even, June 1, September 1, and before Christmas—may suffice.

Yet even this pastoral opinion is not based on any feeling that we can take heaven, take God, take forgiveness, by storm; that by penitential expression we can make Him look with favor on us. The point being labored is that we have to take *ourselves* by storm, in confession and indeed throughout the whole of the spiritual life in which—as we have also said elsewhere herein—we dispose ourselves to accept the grace of God.

Chapter Six

Self-Examination and Confession

BENEFITS FROM the Sacrament of Reconciliation begin before we use it. That is to say, in order to confess our sins we have to know them. To know them we have to seek them. We have to get off by ourselves and, in the help of God from whom no secrets are hid, probe as deeply as possible into our past and present life in the hope of discovering our sins of thought, word, deed, and omission, plus the motives for them. It is well to jot them down on paper as they occur to memory so that in the Confessional itself we may be efficient and workmanlike.

In taking the inventory, whether it be done as cool business or conducted in the heat of shame and tears, one begins to break through the surface of life. Honest self-examination is the initiation fee to an elite group of the human race—those happy few who sincerely set about to "Know Thyself." Apparently it was Socrates who first urged upon the human race this proper study, which has been seconded by all the sages of all eras and cultures, notably including our own. However, despite their unanimous verdict, it has not been widely followed by the mass of mankind. In the main the human race has been content to muddle through, to drift along in life, to waste its sporadic efforts at betterment because it has no known point of attack.

The statement is made in sorrow, not in scorn; we must not be facile here. Self-examination, let alone self-knowledge, is supremely difficult, for in it we actually resist ourselves and are greatly aided in that resistance. This is not merely because in self-examination for Confession we are bringing our sins and not our virtues to view—although everybody who has done it knows how the inevitably partial picture incites rationalization and self-deceit. The real bogeyman seems to be the fear that always inhibits growth. On the beginning level we dread the very process of struggle and growth in which we have deliberately involved ourselves. Who really wants to be different? Different from himself with whom he has finally learned, after some adjustments, to live in decent enough comfort; different from the person his spouse and children and friends have learned to put up with and even to love; different from the prevailing standards of his generation? On a deeper level we humbly fear, and rightly fear, upsetting an apple cart. There is much good in us, even as we now are, and of course we have to "hold fast to that which is good." In the

42

dynamic situation of Confession will we blow everything apart, so that the last state is really worse than the first? We have seen too few psychiatric patients who have been completely put back together again as human wholes with none of their parts missing. Had we not best let sleeping dogs lie? Jung assures us that the well down inside us is deep, and the water murky—who really wants to probe into that? Who really wants brought to the surface of consciousness the things that are (much of the time) "safe" in the subconscious? Doing so has destroyed better people than we are.

Such are some of the inhibiting fears that prevent genuine self-examination, seducing us to settle for an easy and comfortable level of adjustment as in the course of our lives we do what all of us must do—reach for an integrating principle. Since self-examination is also plain hard work, typically we are content to loaf along as near to the surface as we can. For example, when we deal with day-to-day problems our tendency is to see and grapple only with the easily visible circumstances from which a deep-seated issue emerges. We prefer to solve those circumstances on the legalistic or moralistic level (probably leaving a few unsightly fragments to be swept under the rug, but that's life), sigh with relief, and settle back into our easy chairs.

Who will blame us? We are so sufficiently baffled and frustrated by the external circumstances of our daily dilemmas that we are in many ways to be congratulated if we succeed in bringing some sort of order into that chaos. Yet to stop short, say with a legalistic or moralistic capsule, in the solution of human problems is to inhibit the more radical and difficult treatment that can prevent the same things from cropping up again. Circumstances are indeed symptoms, but if the mere symptom is treated no ultimate good is done. The real issue remains, and sooner or later it will break out again in other sets of circumstances. Law and Morality indeed codify long human experience and are good, but being merely good can be the enemy of the best. We must probe inside the capsule to the real and living issue, to the inner spring and heart of things. If we spend our lives dealing with surface events on a surface level, our ancestors might as well have stayed up in the trees.

"The unexamined life is not worth living." Consciousness is what distinguishes human beings from the lesser animals—self-consciousness and consciousness of God—and consciousness is no static matter. Without deep plowing and constant cultivation the weeds choke it, until we are left with an unlived life that is not worth examining. However, to stay with the good side of the matter, a growing human being is a growingly aware, alert, increasingly sentient center of God-consciousness and of self-consciousness (in the good sense of that phrase). The whole spiritual life produces this end, and self-examination is absolutely essential in it. As James Baldwin so truly says, "Whoever cannot tell himself the truth about his past is trapped in it, is immobilized in the prison of his undiscovered self." Baldwin goes on to say, "The artist does, at his best, what lovers do, which is to reveal the beloved to himself and, with that revelation, to make freedom real." In the spiritual life God, the supreme creative artist and lover, does precisely that with us. Our self-examinations are not so dangerous as they might appear, because—as we have insisted—the lover of our souls is with us down there at the depths, gently bringing to view such things as we can then face without disaster. Other matters He lets pass until He has led us to the point where we can bear them. This first benefit of Confession merges almost imperceptibly into a second: in the whole process we becoming increasingly honest, less rationalistic about ourselves. "Oh wad some power the giftie gie us To see oursel' as we are." In self-examination, followed by the process of sacramental confession, He does. This is no light matter, even on the sheerly intellectual front. We have already suggested that the human mind's most facile employment is in rationalization, to the extent that in some ways honesty is the supreme human achievement. Honesty's spiritual synonym, humility, certainly is. To see, to know, and to accept one's self as one truly is in the sight of God—this is the rock foundation upon which the whole structure of Being and Becoming is reared (and, paradoxically, toward which it tends). We enter into real life on hands and knees, through a lowly door—we must die in order to live—we can be filled only when we are empty—we will progress only when we know we haven't yet arrived. No matter what phrase we choose for saying it, humility is being talked about and rightly extolled. The fact is that the spiritual life is best described as "I live, yet not I, but Christ who liveth in me." The living truth is that as we drop off bits and pieces of the Old Man, there is room for the New Man to enter. Once again He comes into the Temple (He spake of the temple of our selves), overthrows the tables of the money changers, and begins cleansing that temple. At the end of this purgative process the initial den of thieves becomes what it properly should be, a house of prayer.

As we move beyond self-examination toward considering the specific benefits of sacramental Absolution, it seems well to mention in passing that in the confessional itself—if our confessor is a skilled director of souls—we may receive some sage advice directed to our particular moral and spiritual situation. The counsel need not be given, and quite often it is not. It does not even need to be implied or suggested in the penance that is requested and imposed, although usually it is. This benefit, in short, should not be overestimated, yet every penitent will join the writer as he pays thankful tribute to several of his confessors and directors. They have helped us profoundly and, we trust, lastingly.

Yet the moral, the intellectual, and the psychological benefits so far discussed amount to very little when we come to the genuine, the truly proper, realm in which the Sacrament of Reconciliation operates—the spiritual. (Here we move worlds beyond the undoubted goods derived from sheerly naturalistic counseling.) Part of the benefit is "negative"—negative, yet of incalculable positive power and truth. We are released from the guilt of our past sins by the direct personal action of God Himself, and we realize the fact with certainty. When we walk out of the church after receiving Absolution, performing our penance, and making our thanksgiving, perhaps we tear our paper list of sins into small bits and throw them into the sewer. It is a most real, most expressive symbolic act.

Some have tried to describe what such "being born again to newness of life" feels like, and in a moment I too will try, first saying that the attempt is an almost impossible endeavor. It feels like different things at different times, even to the same person. Doubtless the emotional response is different in different people, depending upon their psychologies and other factors. Most important of all, "feeling" is not that important anyway. The point is that the downdrag of the past is definitely gone.

In illustration I remember, many years ago, driving across the North American continent dragging behind my car a homemade trailer containing all my worldly goods—all the significant things of the past. The trip was a nightmare of pulling and hauling, with pitifully slow progress. Behind me the whole top-heavy contraption buckled and snapped and creaked. At least daily the trailer hitch would crystallize and break. At the end of each tormented day's progress I dropped weary but tossing into bed, knowing that when I rose the next morning that sinister trailer load would still be waiting for me, firmly and even balefully hitched to my power. For two weeks it was a nemesis I could not be rid of. When I finally clattered into the driveway at my destination, I felt I could not have faced another such day. Mercifully, the trailer was there unloaded piece by piece (the sins confessed one by one, you might say), unhitched, and shoved over into the weeds. When I then headed the car downtown, I felt as if I had jet-assisted takeoff and was proceeding on wings.

Dogmatic theology states that the Sacrament of Reconciliation puts the past behind us and relieves us of the burden of the guilt of our sins. Through my trailer illustration I am trying to say that experience verifies this claim most livingly—that dogma, as always, is a compressed statement of valid religious experience. After confession the conscience is indeed quiet, and the soul is at peace. The recipient really believes in the forgiveness of sins. His conversion is deeply strengthened.

On the positive side, the sacrament definitely releases power for a purposeful future life. Grace is indeed given for living in the experienced presence of God. With this verifiable assertion we have now come to the proper place for making an important observation. Everyone has heard, and possibly has made, the familiar charge that self-examination and confession are inward-turning and morbid practices. The exact opposite seems to be the truth of the matter. Obsession with sin is the morbid thing. Release from this obsession, by the power of absolution, turns us healthily outward.

We may indeed begin to use this sacrament for selfish reasons, as a means of gaining freedom and spiritual ease for ourselves. With continuing use, we do not stay on that trivial level very long. The sacrament becomes a means of objective devotion. That is to say, we may well begin with the glum awareness that "I am a great sinner," but swiftly we realize that "God is a great Saviour," which is the most wonderful discovery we can possibly make.

His absolution is indeed savored most personally, but it is not hugged to one's self. Real grace can never be contained. Quite spontaneously our awe, love, adoration, and magnification of God begin to dominate the scene. We are nicer persons for others to be with; not strange at all, when one really thinks about it. "He increases, and I decrease," even in this most personal and rewarding transaction. The Sacrament of Reconciliation is true worship, in short. Through it we lay our burdens, our only trophies, at His feet and crown Him Lord of all. This true devotion is the most healthy attitude that is possible in life.

To sum up all of the foregoing in one capsule, it may be adequate to say that the Sacrament of Reconciliation supernaturalizes life. The hold of the mere self on self drops away, bit by bit, under the repeated blows against it. The hold of the world, the flesh, and the devil is gradually weakened. The sense of God vastly increases. He is no longer an abstract principle or a "gray blur" somewhere out there. Just as sincere human apology, fully accepted, produces revitalized personal relationship in new deep degree, so in the exchange of love that is the Sacrament of Reconciliation God becomes real—a living, loving, forgiving, and most personal Father. The very world around us comes to be seen in God, seen whole, and therefore is a graceful thing rather than a raw purposeless jumble; so does the world within, that secret self whose secrets are now coming to the light.

In using the Sacrament of Reconciliation one has tasted and seen that God can and will do mighty things, with all loving care. Through it a power for life has entered life from outside, most tangibly, and this presages, even promises, other living intrusions. It is personally known that anything can happen now, and the soul is alert for that happening rather than dull in plodding despair.

Anything can happen? Since God can take away my *sins*, can really separate me from my past and set me loose for the future—since it is really true that He remembers not my sins but remembers ME—there is nothing He cannot do and nothing I cannot be. In His love and power I may actually be able to become the person that in my better moments I sometimes dare to dream about.

In brief, hope is the motive for repentance, and heightened hope is its result. This hope gives to the awakened soul the true interpretation of "Repent ye, for the Kingdom of Heaven is at hand." The phrase is now known as not really a warning and a threat. It is a vibrant promise. "Repent ye—and the Kingdom of Heaven is at hand"!

Chapter Seven

Mental Prayer

AT THIS POINT we have moved from "fasting" to "prayer" by using the bridge of confession, which partakes of the nature of both. Our attention now turns toward some of the elements and a few of the techniques that comprise the other half of the spiritual life.

Naturally, it is impossible even to mention, let alone discuss, all of the fruitful methods of prayer deliberately invented by the spiritual geniuses or spontaneously generated by the personal devotional experience of the saints, which have been found helpful by practical testing in the prayer lives of millions of us common Christians. Out of this vast treasury through which we respond to and appropriate the grace of God, the primary consideration, without any question, is mental prayer. This is true not merely because even a cursory presentation of the subject will document our assertion that systematic spiritual methods, developed and tested by the giants and pygmies of the past, can readily be learned and applied by all of us, to our great enrichment. Nearer to the point is the fact that mental prayer is closely allied to and closely parallels the progression sketched in the analyses or diagrams of the spiritual life presented in Chapter Two. An important aspect of this truth is that the kind of mental prayer a person finds most spontaneously congenial at a given time is the best single gauge, or measure, in the whole life of prayer of the advancement he has so far attained in his spiritual growth. Only the degree of his detachment, or mortification, may outrank it as a touchstone or X ray. For example, the form of mental prayer typical of, and even proper to, the Purgative Way is "discursive meditation." We shall begin with that and move forward along a customary path through "affective" prayer to contemplation, the typical prayer of more advanced states—first noting that this "typicality" is pervasive, reaching into every aspect of the prayer life. That is to say, if one is entering the Illuminative Way and hence probably praying "affectively" in his mental prayer, he will also be spontaneously doing so in intercession or when offering the Eucharist. We shall note this again when we consider these matters.

However, the primary reason for discussing mental prayer first, and at length, is that it includes within itself every other aspect of private prayer. It is almost true to put this statement the other way around and to say that the practice of mental prayer is a complete, private prayer life on its own. In any case we are in the realm of the categorical imperative when we assert the absolute necessity of mental prayer for everybody who has any mental equipment. All the masters of the spiritual life declare with one unanimous voice that meditation is morally necessary to the acquiring of even a low degree of holiness. Fr. Bede Frost states this negatively in *The Art of Mental Prayer* when he writes that it is the "absence of the teaching and practice of mental prayer, with all that it involves, which is the most serious thing in the life of the Church today." When one considers a few other serious matters in the Church's life today this is a strong statement, but Fr. Frost documents his assertion tellingly. We shall shortly attempt to do the same here, from a different point of view, after having made pedantically certain what "discursive meditation" means.

First, however, it will be useful to define some other terms, beginning with the word "prayer" itself. The usual definition given to children is that prayer is "talking with God." A more adult paraphrase is "lifting up the mind to God," or "lifting up the self to God," or "raising the attention to God." The ability to do this is man's greatest gift and leads to his greatest glory. A most rewarding line of thought stems from the horrible realization, "suppose we couldn't pray."

Schematically, "prayer" is divided into "private" and "corporate," or "personal" and "liturgical." Liturgical prayer, corporate prayer, the prayer of the whole Body of Christ, will be discussed a little later on. In this present chapter we are dealing with the aspect of private prayer that is called "mental" because, so to speak, it uses the mind. Since most prayer does, this is somewhat of a misnomer; what is meant by the expression is an emphasis. Vocal prayer, to cite another widely used term, is prayer that uses words—one's own or those of others in which one's aspirations are expressed—but again, most prayer uses words. Mental prayer usually does, so once more what is really meant is an emphasis, or preponderance.

"Affective" prayer, an expression that has also been used here, is prayer that heavily, or preponderantly, offers God our affections or emotions—love, praise, penitence, wonder, gratitude. Usually it does so in words, and generally these occur in short ardent phrases.

We have already defined "contemplation," so at the moment we can end this brief hiatus by noting that the simple act of "raising the attention to God" has been further analysed into a score or more of other rather confusing parts. For example, we read of "The Prayer of Quiet," "The Prayer of Simple Regard," and many others. These categories do have their uses, but the simplest progression that is usually cited—vocal, mental, affective, contemplative—is for most of us a sufficiently sense-making breakdown of the growing prayer life. Far more important, of course, is the prayer life itself. Prayer is learned by praying.

We now return to mental prayer, or rather to that beginning part of it called discursive meditation. This has been defined as the "application of the mind to a supernatural truth, in order to convince ourselves of it, and to be brought to love it by the help of divine grace." It is necessary now to review, in considerable detail, a typical beginning method of discursive meditation—one of many developed in the Church—in order to illustrate this formidable definition in actual living practice. Every reader undoubtedly knows it well already. Doubtless he has studied it, used it, and perhaps even taught it almost *ad nauseam*. Indulgence is asked as we plod over the familiar terrain once again. The reasons for doing this are compelling and will shortly appear.

Assuming that the meditation is to be made in the morning at a time and place rigorously blocked off for this purpose (the assumption brings up a host of considerations that would fill a chapter by themselves), brief "remote" preparation is made for it the evening before. At that time we at least determine the subject that will be thought and prayed about the next day. A short passage from the Gospels—a self-contained incident, not a whole chapter—is always good subject matter. The beginner will do well to work straight through one of the Synoptic Gospels, event by event, thus immersing himself in the Sacred Humanity of our Lord.

In the morning, after the flesh, the world, and the devil have been somewhat subjugated, "proximate" preparation is made. Some of us found it useful to stand quietly for a short time at a little distance from the place of prayer, collecting our laughable wits, unifying our pitiful selves, beginning to achieve a touch of surface quiet. We then approached the holy ground, knelt silently for a few moments, and let the self sink into deeper stillness. We can all recall that on some occasions this was managed quite simply; on others, detailed discipline was required, such as mentally starting at the head and moving slowly down to the feet, quieting each part of the body *en route.*

After that we "realized the presence of God." It is everlastingly important to remember that "putting one's self in the presence of God" is not accomplished by vivid forced imagination. We cannot reach up to heaven and pull God down—herein lies pretty much the whole distinction between religion and magic. All we should aspire to do is make an effort of attention and will, which perform their offices whether or not God becomes palpably present in response. In short, "God's presence" is not a subjective hallucination produced by our efforts and available to our feelings. Any attempt in this direction, including such attempts via chemistry, is fraught with disaster. Always our part is to desire, warmly or coldly as the case may be. God is the sole judge, and the only dispenser, of the response.

(It may well be observed parenthetically that in "practicing the presence of God" one not only looks toward him quite gently and rather swiftly, but it is also important to do so in one's own most natural way. Some people turn spontaneously toward God the Father—toward the transcendent and numinous

Person "up there," who will always for them be primarily "up there." Others focus on God the Son who is for them God "over there" across the room or even—this was my own way, I confess without embarrassment—in the wall six inches in front of their noses. Still others realize God the Holy Spirit deep within themselves, the Ground of their being. Almost everyone finds the Real Presence most readily in the Blessed Sacrament Reserved, but this is not always available even in the parish church, and certainly not in our own bedrooms. Wherever we are and however we do it, the point is to slip off our shoes and affirm, without strain, that we are on holy ground.)

A final act of faith, an act of humility, and a petition for grace to pray well are then useful to many. With these dispositions made we sit back and begin the meditation itself by exercising the memory. We recall the subject on which we had chosen to dwell. When memory is reluctant to cooperate, we resist our impulses to irritation and simply reread the selected passage. (If you can't remember what *that* was to be, just choose another.)

To cast all this into the past tense, where doubtless it properly belongs, we then deliberately pictured the scene of action by giving free rein to the imagination. We saw, felt, and heard it in all its detail, not remotely and impersonally as an idle spectator, but with our selves right there in the living heart of things. When the Passion was our subject, we stood at the foot of the cross on Good Friday's dark afternoon, watching, listening, and taking part with friend and foe and neutral. We were in the boat with our Lord and His other disciples on the stormy lake, when that was the scene. Participating reality, by means of vivid imagination controlled by the actual events, was greatly to be desired at this beginning stage in mental prayer.

When, finally, "we were there" we exercised the intellect. We reflected and reasoned upon the event, bending our minds attentively to it. Sometimes we realized that far more rumination was possible to us, with the episode isolated and "held still" before our undivided attention, than was available to the original disciples in the days of our Lord's physical presence among them. With them an incident flashed by, while we were privileged to concentrate in depth. We were happy to seize this opportunity to the utmost of our ability, realizing that the importance of our mentation could hardly be exaggerated.

Up to this point, of course, prayer had not yet begun, for prayer is the lifting of the attention to God. After or during the mental attention, however, true prayer did start—either spontaneously on an alert morning or by deliberate effort on an arid one. Whatever the subjective condition might be, in good time we began to pray, using all the various parts or moods of prayer in connection with the subject that was before us. We adored the divine goodness we had come to see; we humbled ourselves before the Great Example in front of our eyes; we exercised praise, thanksgiving, petition, intercession, wonder, self-giving, desire, all as the scene before our mind's eye called forth these responses. When the prayer flagged, which it did, we went back to the imagined scene and to further pondering upon it. Then the prayer rose, or was raised, again.

That was the very heart of the whole act of mental prayer as practiced in discursive meditation. We went on thus until our time was up, moving back and forth between the picture and the prayer.

The conclusion of it all was concise and clear, but vitally important. A definite resolution was made, either to avoid something or to do something, that day. The "something" was, naturally, in connection with the subject and the desire that had been occupying the attention during the past fifteen minutes or the past half hour. The resolution—to write that delayed letter; to recite the Creed at noon; to keep one's temper in an approaching appointment— obviously brought the will into play, ensuring that we were not merely indulging in a rosy glow of escapist unreality. The prayer would be tested in its later fruits, where prayer must always be tested.

Finally, with an act of thanksgiving for the grace received in the meditation, with petition to keep the resolution, and perhaps with an Our Father for some special intention or for the final fun of it, we rose and went. Sometimes we did depart most reluctantly, with many a backward glance and the fervent realization that it had been good for us to have been there. More often we burst forth with the relief of a boy let out of school.

With that behind us we are in a position to distinguish several important levels on which discursive meditation operates—after making the important observation that the entire religious life is engaged in primarily for the glory of God. It centers on Him rather than on ourselves. Indeed, in our religious climate with its strong bias toward individualism and subjectivism, there is no possibility of asserting too strongly and too often, with Fr. Frost, "the truth that all our spiritual exercises are means toward seeking and knowing God, and not for our pleasure and comfort." We must be quite unrelaxing about our efforts to move ourselves, and if that is our business, to move others above the stage of the love of God for the sake of his gifts to the heights where God is loved for God. Yet, for all that, the spiritual life *is* supremely creative of personality, so we will risk a seeming selfishness and note what meditation does for us.

1.—It makes us acquainted with the sheer blunt facts, just as any diligent continuous study of any topic does. Through daily study of the Gospel story, incident by incident, we come to know that story in its factual fullness. We also learn the Creed, the Lord's Prayer, the Beatitudes, many psalms, many hymns, and all the other things that have been the subjects of meditation. Familiarity with these building blocks, the facts, is always basic and seems to be needed in our modern Christian world. Facts are static things, it is true.

They have never moved the human race to action, and they never will. Nevertheless they are the essential raw material when we begin dynamically to build. Some towering structures have, unfortunately, been built without this solid foundation.

2.—Meditation trains what used to be called the "faculties"—the memory, the imagination, the reason, the will, the concentration—because in it they receive systematic exercise. A person with a disciplined mind does risk frustration in fuzzy company, but that too can be good for his soul.

3.—Meditation "lifts up our eyes unto the hills" and exposes God to us. To state this in reverse, it exposes us to the great themes, the great ideas, the great visions, the great human stirrings, instead of the trivialities that can so easily occupy us. We have meditated upon Faith, Hope, Love, Patience, Courage and all the other magnificent obsessions of the human race. Because we have done so in a vital context, using not merely the intellect but also the emotions and the will, these things begin to take up their living abode in us. They begin to move us dynamically.

4.—This movement is accelerated because meditation "unpacks" these things and makes them our own. The teachings of the Church are not arbitrary inventions of a dyspeptic hermit after a bad night, sadistically foisted upon the world in the hope of giving it a headache too. They express in words— inadequate ones, but the least inadequate ones available—the deepest truths in the world, as these truths have been existentially perceived by geniuses and validated in the living experience of millions. Doctrine is, in short, truth packed for transportation across the centuries. Meditation unpacks this suitcase, unties this bundle, cracks this shell of words, as few other ways of knowing can. It vastly enables personal, living, participating knowledge of reality.

5.—Furthermore, meditation peels the onion of these truths, leading us to ever deeper understanding, through this participation, of the heights and depths of reality. For example, last year the beginner thought he knew what "descended into hell" means, but this morning God found opportunity to show him a hitherto unnoticed avenue in the labyrinth. He followed down that track a bit, staring at this and that, until he recoiled in horror and went back. Some day he may go that way again, but meanwhile he knows that what he knew last year was merely surface, and he more than suspects that his present fearsome knowledge is only the beginning. Prior to this morning he had only heard with the hearing of the ears, but now his eyes have seen somewhat.

6.—Therefore he stands in awe and sins not—meditation syncretizes, or makes whole; is creative of a *person*. In example, we can remember that once upon a time you and I had many isolated talents. We worked for this or that additional skill or virtue. We came to know a smattering of astronomy, something about salesmanship, a dash of literature, a little philosophy, and a host of other splintered subjects, abilities, and avocations, including how to barbecue a chicken for our friends. All of these are being smoothly gathered into one nowadays because, of course, *we* are. To express this somewhat differently, once I was a son, a father, and a husband. Now, by exposure to the Trinity in Unity, I find myself slowly becoming a *person,* whose varying facets are merging into one.

7.—Similarly, meditation intertwines religion and life, to the point that religion is no longer merely a reasonably important part of life but is life itself. Indeed, as a result of systematic discursive meditation, religion—reunion with God—is glimpsed as being the only whole life. Union with God and the certain promise of ever closer union with him is seen as all that really matters. As a fruit of mental prayer Jesus is becoming one's Way, one's Truth, even one's Life.

8.—Meditation not only "peels the onion of truth" in depth, as sketched previously, but also broadens the view of truth horizontally, as it were. It presses back the blinders that are standard human equipment so that we see vast areas we had never dreamed existed. This knack, or gift, of seeing to new horizons and thinking on many planes all at the same time becomes a part of life. Learned in meditation, abetted by mortification, it spreads throughout the unifying self. Gradually, as we have indicated in another context, the whole of nature becomes sacramental for us. Often, if not always, it is an outward and visible sign of inward and spiritual grace. Our space and time are being sanctified. We marvel at our blindness back at the beginning, when only the most gigantic intrusions could reach us, for we know that our present vision sees things as they really were all the time. The darkness that formerly lay over the land is being dispelled by detachment and mental prayer, so that the true shape of things is emerging.

All this can be pulled together in the statement that mental prayer is basic in the development of spiritualized human personality because it increases awareness by (1) bringing reality to our attention and (2) assimilating it livingly.

What is "the development of human personality" but the absorption of God into it, with an inevitable "increase of awareness"? On the personal level the two phrases are quite identical in meaning. "Increase of awareness" seems to differ from "development of personality" only when society is, only when other people are, brought into view; but really it does not even differ there.

The truth of the matter is the basic theme consistently urged herein: that the truly developed person is one of those too rare upthrust individuals who spontaneously, by reason of his very existence, increases the awareness of his whole generation and of the generations that will come after him. He is truly creative. In him the sun rises at the dawning of a new day, and the Illumination cannot avoid spreading. As has been stated already, the truly gigantic personalities of history—Moses, Buddha, Socrates, and all the others in the reader's favorite list—are always Promethean. They were in living touch with reality and able to communicate it. They were ladders set up between earth and heaven, upon which the very angels of God ascended and descended, bringing gifts to men. Their story is the truly significant history of mankind. By comparison all the rest—the clash of empires, the strife of kings—is pathetic sound and fury, signifying nothing. Mary has chosen the better part, not only for herself but for all. Like another and a greater Mary, she is the one who brings Christ into the world.

The solitary unknown soul diligently making his daily meditation in a quiet country village or a teeming city tenement is, doubtless, no new Dante. Yet he is different from the mass of people, whom we meet by the hundreds every day. Most of them don't matter very much. They might almost as well be trees walking. Every now and then, however, we meet that genuine article, the saint or the near saint, and we know in the experience the power of a life devoutly lived. It may be that our contact with him lasts only a few minutes, but the influence of that holy soul is enduring and profound in us. He is contagious of his interior vitality. Having seen him we have, in some degree, been aware that he has been with Jesus of Nazareth. Thus, having seen him we have in some degree seen the Father. In our hearts we say "Truly this was a son of God," and we ourselves go out to be and do again, renewed in higher purpose once more.

In that living person, in that rare yet familiar experience, is seen the real necessity of mental prayer.

The method of meditation outlined above is a heavily discursive one, chosen for analysis here because it illustrated sound, beginning practice and introduces some indispensable topics. Another equally familiar method needs brief sketching now, because as we progress in mental prayer the discursive methods begin to pall. They bore us. There is no desire in them; we have plodded through all that ground before. Now we want to fly swiftly over the intervening land and be at once with God in intimate colloquy.

Augustine Baker even writes, quite correctly, of the actual "misery of souls that are tied to a prayer improper to them." The point is stressed because many good people, motivated by misdirected loyalty and obedience, try to continue with a method of mental prayer that binds them to great chunks of intellectualizing. They sense that their prayer is being inhibited rather than enabled by it, and yet they linger on. They must realize that it isn't the subtlety of our imagining and reasoning that matters—we can easily be deluded about this—but the prayer that is thereby called forth. Our second familiar method is of a type that recognizes, and enables, this development.

In using it the "remote" and the "proximate" preparations are much the same as before, as is the concluding thanksgiving, but these supporting elements now usually do their work with the swiftness of accustomed ease. When and if they do, they should be curtailed; there is no need to whip a willing and alert horse. What really differs, however, is the structure of the body of this way of mental prayer. It can be well stated in three phrases: Jesus before the eyes, Jesus in the heart, Jesus in the hands. Here we are close to the heart of things. As M. Olier so truly says, "Christianity consists in three points . . . to regard Jesus, to be united to Jesus, to work in Jesus. . . . The first is called adoration; the second, communion; the third, cooperation."

Let us say we have chosen to meditate on the subject of humility. First, then, we see that virtue illustrated in and by Jesus. Quite rapidly, yet with lingering love, we let pass before our mind's eye such pictures as Jesus in the Bethlehem manger; Jesus washing the disciples' feet at the Last Supper; Jesus's hidden thirty years in a remote village; Jesus dying on the cross; and any other illustrations of our Lord's humility as readily suggest themselves. We have the facts now, and these facts come readily to mind. There is no need to analyze the situation closely any more; we have done all that many times before. Now all we need do is look at them, pass them in review. Indeed, that is all we want to do. We prefer to adore Jesus, rather than merely think about Him.

Since the human mind cannot pay attention to two matters at the same time; cannot, simultaneously, both think and adore; our thinking (better, our *looking*) is usually abandoned quite soon. We begin to pour forth our prayers to God. In ardent communion we express our praise, wonder, penitence, thanksgiving, as these are called forth by the magnificence of God and the contrast of our shriveled selves. Finally, thanks to the concluding act of the will, the divine virtue takes deeper root in us and is shown forth in His world. Thus we acquire it in the living of it.

M. Olier has shown us that this apparently simple but very searching and quite fervent method of prayer conforms precisely to "Hallowed by Thy Name; Thy Kingdom come; Thy will be done." With the introduction of these short zealous phrases as the developing, simplifying soul's now spontaneous, preferred, and most natural way of expressing itself, we have come to affective Prayer.

Augustine Baker, in his classic *Holy Wisdom*, includes many suggestions for these "acts of affective prayer"—prayer, in all its modes, offered in short, sharp darts. These bursts of prayer, sometimes forced and sometimes spontaneous, can consist of a single word, or a brief phrase, or even a whole sentence—a verse from a psalm, for example. The choice, or the expression, depends on so many delicate factors that we recoil from analysis.

Augustine Baker is such a preeminent apostle of affective prayer that at this transition point—contemplation lies just over the horizon—we suggest a third method of mental prayer, derived from Baker, who in his turn got it from Blosius. The similarities with, and the differences from, the method just described should be closely noted: "Without much discoursing to represent to the mind any mystery to which the soul has an affection (as our Lord's agony, or *Ecce Homo*, or His dereliction on the cross, etc.) and to regard Him in such a state with as much tenderness of affection as may be, exercising short acts of love, compassion, gratitude, and so forth."

"Short acts of love, compassion, gratitude, and so forth"—which we then keep up pretty much all day long. This is affective prayer. It is also a loving and almost total "recollection." When this becomes the habitual way of prayer, a person has reached the point beyond which he can no longer meditate at all, and he most definitely should not try to.

In his spiritual development he has come to the so-called "ligature," on the other side of which mental prayer, in the usual sense of those words, is impossible. Only contemplation (if "only" is the proper modifier) is available to him. He stands on the threshold of direct, immediate worship of God. For a while, as he is passing over the threshold, there can be some alternation between affective prayer and contemplation—there can be some deliberate use of, say, that third method on days when contemplation is impossible—but essentially the ligature forces the end of meditation.

The more analytical of our spiritual masters, when dealing with this fact, attempt to describe the spiritual situation in which meditation must be abandoned for the soul's good. For example, according to Augustine Baker we are being called to Contemplation when (1) we are at peace with God as to former sins and have in general no present affection to "creatures" (that is to say, are almost perfectly detached) and (2) we experience a certain disgust with meditation. St. John of the Cross, in various places throughout his writings, gives several tests differing slightly from one another, but they are similar enough to be combined into a threefold sign: (1) meditation becomes unsatisfying, dry, and actually impossible; (2) there is no inclination to fix the sense on particular objects, exterior or interior; (3) the soul delights to be alone with God, without any particular considerations, in inward peace. (Naturally, it is terribly important that all three of these signs be concurrently present. If only one or two of them are, we are merely victims of carelessness, distractions, lukewarmness, acedia, or plain laziness.)

In a labored commentary on the fact of the ligature, I go back and take a running start from a point mentioned earlier: that we can really attend to only one thing at a time. For example again, we can *think* or we can *pray*, but we cannot do both simultaneously.

Prayer is, as we have said, the lifting up of the attention to God. At the start of our journey from a beginning state of nearly total distraction and earthboundness toward our final goal of complete recollection and heavenly dwelling, much "spurning down" and "lifting up" have to be done. Time is the mercy of eternity, and as we begin to use time for its eternal purposes we sanctify small portions of it. For example, we deliberately lift up our minds to God, usually in vocal prayer, each morning and again each night. As the years go by we increase the frequency of this orientation. We begin to pray at noon also, then at lesser intervals, then every hour, and so on.

In further example, when engaged in mental prayer we at first use many props, or levers, or "aids to lifting" in those heavily discursive methods of meditation. Most of our time then is spent disposing ourselves to prayer, and very little in the prayer itself. Mostly we are attending to our thoughts about God, and only because of that are we able to attend, on fitful occasion, to God Himself. During these flashes we stop thinking and begin praying. However, we are unable to maintain this level of union very long. Shortly we become distracted, fall back to earth, and have to repeat the process.

Nevertheless, as we persevere in our detachment from "creatures" and our attachment to the Creator, it becomes easier and easier to pray. Less and less thinking will suffice to lift the attention to God. Finally the soul flies to Him as readily as a bird to the fowler. And ultimately one is in constant recollection, which makes possible the prayer of contemplation. In this prayer one does not think at all. One does not attend to symbols at all. In fact one voids oneself of them and attends solely to God Himself. To put this another way, one has been enabled by God to transcend reason, which is not the final, let alone the only, means of union between the human and the divine.

The immense importance of the union of our minds with the 'mind' of God—of, as it were, our thinking His thoughts and letting His world view more and more become ours—needs no further stress here. Reason is a genuine unitive faculty, God-given to lead us toward Himself, but it isn't our only means of contact with Truth, Beauty, and Goodness. Prayer, that lifting of our beings toward God, concentrating on Him, letting His Spirit intimately infuse ours, is a unitive process in its own right. There is also an ineffable one-ing, an inexpressible, unitive process beyond the reach of thought and of active prayer, which is the union of love. Additionally, there is that to which everything leads: the total union of will, of character, of the whole human person with the divine.

The above has been stated from our point of view: upward from the human toward God. We need to remember that God effects His desire to unite Himself with us, hence that the viewpoint can and must be turned around. God gives and enables those beginning means of union in the first place, and at the proper prepared time seems to bestow still another, continuous with the ones below it but surpassing them. He seems to infuse a new "mind," or way of union—alas that words fail—in us when this gift can be received. Early spiritual writers would probably incline to say that an *old* "mind"—the completed unitive apparatus of Adam before the Fall—is rebestowed and reattained; that "original integrity," shattered by "original sin," is restored by grace.

However that may be, at this point one's great effort is to let the new-formed "mind" have free scope—is to press down under a "cloud of forgetting" all those things that used to be great aids to union, but which are now distractions. They must lie quietly forgotten. The imagination is especially hard to pacify, so one usually has to throw it a bone; a short single word like "God" or "Love" or "Sin," or a brief affective phrase, or the Jesus Prayer to gnaw on. One is then more free to press upward through the mists toward invisible God.

The Cloud of Unknowing states the matter thus:

For ever when thy mind is occupied with any bodily thing, be it to never so good an end, yet thou art beneath thyself in this working, and without thy soul. And ever when thou feelest thy mind occupied with the subtle conditions of the powers of thy soul and their workings in ghostly things, as be vices or virtues, of thyself or of any creature that is ghostly and even with thee in nature, to the end that thou mightest by this work learn to know thyself and further thy perfection; then thou art within thyself and even with thyself. But ever when thou feelest thy mind occupied with no manner of thing that is bodily or ghostly, but only with the very substance of God, then thou art above thyself and beneath thy God.

When the ligature occurs (when our atrophied contemplative powers come back to life?), the elastic band of our trained attention—detached from earth and attached to heaven—snaps us toward God. It may be useful to point out that a contemplative's earthly mind has not been destroyed by the setting free, above it as it were, of a heavenly one. On the contrary he can, outside of prayer while he is attending to other things, dictate a letter, compose a symphony, create an epic, or guide the destinies of nations far better and more easily than most others. To use a lesser illustration, he can read the words of a fine prayer with complete understanding and savor. He is attending to it on the plane of literary composition. But *in* prayer, in contemplation, he simply cannot conduct a discursive meditation. He is then attending to God Himself, not to thoughts about God. He cannot, in prayer, use a fine vocal expression with any understanding at all. The Lord's Prayer to him then is meaningless. He is not attending to it. He is on a different wavelength.

The Cloud of Unknowing expresses all of the above, and much more, quite simply: "God cannot be thought, He can only be loved."

I have indicated earlier that we spiritual beginners are warned, and with wisdom are warned, against studying treatises about Illumination, Contemplation, Union, and the Mystical Life. There is enough work, confusion, and potential despair in the labor of the Purgative Way to keep us all sufficiently occupied in the present without being distracted or overwhelmed by a foretaste of what is yet to come. At the same time it seems well for all to have a general awareness of the road ahead—to know that while all the acts and exercises, the activities and methods, the applications and diligences of the Purgative Way are essential to spiritual development, nevertheless ultimately they will be largely abandoned. Because this becomes especially clear through the consideration of mental prayer, we stress the now familiar topic at this point.

First, by reiterating that in its normal development the mental prayer of those of us who are actively involved in the world begins with discursive meditation and ends with affective prayer, much as we have sketchily outlined above. The great majority of us never come to enjoy contemplation, save in occasional flashes. It would seem that God cannot call us to this activity because our strenuous participation in a hurly-burly world inhibits the possibility. There have indeed been many mystics and contemplatives on American soil, but most of us in the Western world do not have the courage or the opportunity to break through the sound barrier in the manner, say, of Thoreau. The best we can hope to do under our circumstances is to make our diligent meditations. There can be little or no infused prayer until, after death, we are called up higher, where we cannot heal the sick, nor bury the dead, nor teach the ignorant, because there are no such there. In that state, freed from strenuous involvement in horizontal affairs like "corporal works of mercy" and even "spiritual works of mercy," we will all become contemplatives, for the Vision of God is Heaven, and the sole activity thereof.

Yet it may be that the "leisure society" with which we are threatened will produce some basic changes, rendering obsolete the unanimous verdict of the spiritual masters of past centuries who so truly state that contemplation, in the Church Militant, is an extremely rare vocation. Certainly those who come to retirement will do very well to put their withdrawal pains to spiritual use, seeking and desiring in them to learn if God will call them to contemplative or even unitive prayer in this life, as the crown and glory of their diligent decades in the Purgative and Illuminative Ways.

There is no reason why they should have to enter a monastery to make this search. They could simply choose their own Walden, and there let supernature take its course. Even if the call to contemplation did not come, the cultivation of eternity would be a good devotion of their final earthly years. Certainly the Church, in setting up its retirement facilities, seems bound to make opportunity for spiritual life a major consideration. Surely in some of the Church's retirement homes the full Liturgy should be available, along with an adequate library, a competent director, and a whole ethos-and-event pointing toward and enabling the contemplative life. One hopes for pilot-plant retirement colonies of this sort, if only to learn whether this would crown an entire civilization.

To return to the main track, with apologies for the ramble: at some point, here or hereafter, the whole apparatus of the Purgative Way will be left behind, for the good is ever the enemy of the best. A formerly indispensable ladder would be an encumbrance to one who has mastered the vaulting pole. To state this more truly—in the mysterious interplay of divine omnipotence and human free will, the best we can build toward Heaven turns out to be a tower of Babel. The Holy City is always let down from above. Universal experience testifies that in the developing spiritual life our own activity yields progressively to God's until His becomes the vastly dominant factor—yet our activity must first have been there to prepare the way for His. John the Baptist, that essential forerunner, said it best: "He must increase, but I must decrease."

Hence we venture to stress that contemplation may be waiting for us—after long years of rigorous diligence in the active exercises of the Purgative Way, and on the other side of the Dark Night of the Soul. Activity will produce the beginnings of being. It will develop many essential faculties and powers—like intellect, will, emotion, memory—and then these very things will have to be given up at last. There comes a time when they are of no avail and are even contrary to avail. They actually come to stand in the way of God, doubtless because they are part of the self and hence have to die too, along with everything else. When these things begin to be acted upon, when the soul is powerless and the sledgehammer blows fall on its painful inertness, then it is time to lift up the eyes and look about. When a virtue becomes an imperfection, when a stile becomes a fence, when a trusted power turns impotent, when the developed self stands in the way of the real self, then God is probably saying, "Not by might . . . but by My spirit."

At that time, one should seek out a good director instead of continuing to fight on in despairing aloneness trying to make one's impossible meditations.

Until that time, one should continue them with the greatest diligence, resisting every diabolic blandishment to the contrary, including the above words.

Chapter Eight

Devotional Reading

IN THE "Desert Island" game, played strictly according to Hoyle, we select the one book we would take into exile if necessity thus stripped us down. (My own choice would be a composite wherein the Bible and the Prayer Book are bound up within one set of covers. Obviously this involves as much cheating as selecting a one-volume edition of Shakespeare.) We all play the game from time to time in its various nonpurist forms, because we have found it a good device for estimating the measure of selfhood, independent of external props, we have so far attained.

Playing it solitaire recently, with a view to discovering the more traditional means of grace I might be able to lose without irreparable loss, I concluded I could manage without sermons, stained glass, music, statuary, retreats, Stations of the Cross, and a host of other beloved and gracious things. I am delighted I used to have them all, and thankful that I still have a lot of them, but none of them looms as essential any more. Some day, I trust, all of these and many other means of grace will become not merely superfluous but actually distracting. We can all look forward to, or at least hope for, that distant time when symbols and images have finally come to stand in the way of clear sight.

On the positive side, the game reaffirmed the primacy of Liturgy—Eucharist and Office—as not only the first spiritual essential but the one that will never pass away on this side of the grave. After it has accomplished its beginning work of bringing reality and translating reality—as it were from outside of us—it remains reality itself in which we engage. Deprived of it, we would be utterly lost and doubtless would soon find ourselves wandering down inviting sideroads that peter out in deadly swamps or sudden precipices. However, because liturgical prayer will be discussed elsewhere in this book, we can soon dismiss the subject here.

After liturgy the second most important means of grace seemed to be devotional reading, whose connection with mental prayer is so intimate that its consideration comes naturally at this point. Devotional reading ranked in high place as far into the future as prevision could see, for surely I shall always be unable to take in reality raw. Some spiritual mother must always digest, or at least cook, it for me.

Obviously I may be combining "first" and "second" here, because liturgy

66

does include spiritual reading on the highest possible plane. The Bible is the best devotional reading in the world, and the finest way to read it is in the context of the Eucharist and the daily offices of Morning and Evening Prayer. The lectionary's assignment of psalms and lessons not only gives selectivity—the Bible does not lend itself equally to devotional reading, or to any other kind of reading, for that matter—but also during at least half the year the Church's mind is impressed on the chosen passages and expressed through them. Early "types" of eternal "mysteries" are presented to us in vital context. Thus, interpretative and guiding overtones are written in for us, as it were, and we are led to see more than meets the unaided eye. For example, on Good Friday the assigned Old Testament reading tells of Abraham's call, or temptation, to sacrifice his son Isaac. On the Feast of our Lord's Transfiguration we read of Moses coming down from Mt. Sinai with blindingly glowing face after being with God. On Pentecost we are pointed to the tale of the confusion of tongues at Babel and realize that Pentecost reversed this. (Incidentally, there comes a time when the daily use of the offices should be given thorough trial. For many people this personal use of the Church's prayer combines offering, food, stability, insight, and solace in a remarkable manner. In our present context of spiritual reading, let me merely extol the fact that the lectionary leads us skillfully through the best passages in the Old Testament at least once a year; that it exposes us to the entire New Testament twice every year; and that it absolutely immerses us in the Psalter. For an investment of some twenty minutes a day this is quite a bargain.)

If we can legitimately separate liturgy and reading, however, I fondly imagine that given these two ways of bringing reality to me and me to reality, I could manage spiritually. Perhaps I am wrong and would speedily find myself floundering without certain other elements in my accustomed observances—loss of the mighty rhythms of the Christian Year would be especially dangerous—but I would be willing to try a desert island some day with only Omar's provisions. A loaf of bread, a jug of wine, and a book of verses might indeed prove to be paradise.

Rumination of this sort leads naturally into trying to select the particular books for devotional reading that would be "musts" on any satisfactory list. It is quickly seen that this can only be done with one's self in view, for one man's meat is so often another's poison that it is impossible to dogmatize on the subject. St. Augustine's *Confessions* may be fine for me but leave you cold. The same, or the reverse, might well be the situation in regard to *The Imitation of Christ*. My bedside table always holds *The Cloud of Unknowing*, whereas Kelly's *Testament of Devotion* might be more at home on yours. So also it would be, surely, with Fenelon, Grou, de Caussade, St. Teresa, Pascal, or St. Francis de Sales. When you come down to it, spiritual reading is the kind that inspirits a particular person.

The point that stands out most sharply in the above illustrative enumeration is the classic nature of books for truly devotional reading. There are indeed good modern productions in this line—Evelyn Underhill, Olive Wyon, Simone Weil, and Father Andrew come immediately to mind, as do C. S. Lewis, Chesterton, E. B. White, Thoreau, and many others, for of such is the Kingdom of Heaven too—but the entire list, ancient and modern, cannot be long, because a true spiritual gem is a million-to-one shot. Before a book can speak *cor ad cor* two considerations have to be satisfied: its author must have probed reality in depth, and he must have expressed his personal knowledge in such a way that truth is conveyed. Either one of these abilities is extremely rare; their combination in one person is almost nonexistent. Such a person has successfully solved that fundamental, two-sided human problem we have isolated—to know truth and to communicate truth—and few there be who achieve that. Hence, the wise course is to stay with the classics and with just a chosen few of them.

Once we have come to our choices, we should give high priority to doing some reading in them every day. To facilitate this we will be well advised to keep one of our books at our bedside, another on the end table beside our favorite chair, and still another at our prayer desk or in our quiet corner. Thus the midnight moments, the odd moments, the vacant moments, and the times we are dry in meditation are provided against. By simply picking up and reading, we can move swiftly into another world and have that world enter into us.

The secular reading and study we all must somehow accomplish is essential, is good, and yet is one more strand in the cable binding us to things temporal. By it our standards and judgments are conformed to this world only—surely we are more tied to earth by necessary and worthy affairs than we are by evil influences. Devotional reading, far from being one more overwhelming chore to be somehow accomplished, is the antidote to all that. A spiritual classic leads us to think with eternity once again. We begin reading it, and almost immediately its light shines in our darkness. True values seep back into us. We realize we have been wandering in a barren and dry land, thirsty, restless, gasping for air. We see that the dust kicked up by daily duty had cut off the long view. The spiritual classic, coming straight and clear from the mountain top, brings a wind from home. It recalls us to the real. Our whole mood changes. We are refreshed beyond words.

This is so, not merely because of the matter that it brings to our souls but also because of the manner in which this is done. The manner or style of a spiritual classic is at one with reality just as its content is. The writers listened so closely to the music of the spheres that they became attuned to fine expression. Because they lived down at the heart of reality, they thought and wrote in keeping. Their words and phrases speak literally, allegorically, symbolically, and anagogically all at once, because they saw reality on all its planes simultaneously and could not refrain from expressing it that way. As we read them, noting how they make familiar fact glow with the most startling overtones of meaning, we are guided and trained to think in the same manner.

We are, that is to say, if we read the classics in the way they were written. This is not "a chapter a day." Horizontal extent is never the goal. Nor is merely *slow* reading, although slow reading closes in on the point. Certainly "speed reading" is an absolute waste of time in this field. That skill should be reserved for the writing that merits the treatment.

Spiritual reading must be done as in a creative situation, where the reader is an alert respondent. The author labored to have something to say and to say it. He packed his sentences full and running over, so that his every word deserves pondering, both for what it is in itself and for what it connotes. We must read not so much slowly as deeply, with much underlining, circling, and marking of the page. We must immerse ourselves until the reality in the words has awakened reality in our hearts.

Then we will want to go back and start over again, whereupon we will note with astonishment that our previous understanding was only on the surface. We hadn't really seen what was said, after all.

This is why a few books will suffice. The same spiritual classic can easily be read a dozen different times, yielding a dozen new veins of treasure—all of which were there all the time patiently waiting for the reader's eyes to open. It bears repeating that our eyes open, our comprehension develops, in great part because in the spiritual reading itself we are exposed to the thought processes of true maturity and hence begin to absorb them.

In one over-used word, spiritual reading is done *prayerfully*, with the prayer being more the end result than the beginning attitude. Indeed the whole art of mental prayer seems to have begun, historically, with spiritual reading, and for many souls it certainly ends that way. In truly devotional reading we are making a meditation after the classic form of reading—thinking—praying. The reading sparks the thinking, and the thinking calls forth the praying, so spontaneously that we do not usually notice the inevitable sequence. The written words are a true means of grace. Reality called them into being, and reality resides in them. When our flint meets that steel a spark flies, kindling a flame. We lift our eyes from the page and stare unseeing. Our minds begin churning. Speedily our penitence, praise, thanksgiving, wonder, desire, and adoration begin rising. In the beginning the word was with God, and now, because of the word, we are.

Chapter Nine

Corporate Prayer

I ONCE HAD the astonishing experience of receiving a long-distance telephone call from a young man who asked if he could come to live for a while in my town so that, as he put it, I could teach him Christianity. The conversation and subsequent correspondence showed him to be an unusual person, greatly gifted and far along in spiritual growth. Although he had been born in the Western world, his religious knowledge and development stemmed from years of living and studying in the Orient—during one long period he had stayed in a Tibetan monastery. He knew nothing whatever about Christianity, however, and he wanted to learn.

I declined letting him come simply because he could not have found in my parish what he was seeking. The religious observances available in our corporate life were not at that time sufficiently rich to express and convey the fullness for which he was ready and which he deserved. In sorrow, mixed with some envy, I referred him to another place where a far more adequate life was available.

Part of the point here is the simple but vastly important truth that Christianity cannot be taught as in a lecture course, by words. Christianity knows well that all real education, all growth, comes by participation. Even when The Word Himself was on earth He did not rely too much on words. His primary call, always, was "Come, follow Me." He made disciples—people under discipline who in the living of His life, in the doing of His will, learned His doctrine. His new Body the Church has always continued steadfastly in the same manner, stressing the life of "fellowship, and . . . breaking of bread . . . and prayers."

The writer is now under strong temptation to stray into the area of Christian education, demonstrating with every resource at command the absolute priority of Christianity's corporate life in this field. The temptation will be partially resisted, but the reader is asked to keep this allied matter in the back of his mind as we progress. We will remain with our primary topic, or rather return to it by saying that the spirituality so far presented has perhaps—in spite of every effort to the contrary—seemed individualistic or even private. Certainly the time has come when it must be stated in so many words that there is no such thing as a "private" Christian spirituality. There is not even such a thing as a "bipolar spirituality," which alternates between the private and the corporate, between the personal and the liturgical, with each of these atoning for the lacks of the other. It is all one, and it is all corporate. Christian spirituality is brought to us by the Body of Christ, is learned by living the corporate life of that body, and is engaged in for corporate purposes—for the further strengthening of the Body from which we derived it, for impingement on the world in which that Body lives as leaven or shines as light, and hence for the greater honoring of God by His whole creation. It is not alone in this, of course. Everywhere we look in life—including, *par excellence*, religion—we see that no man stands alone. Everywhere we see the same identical situation: we must all come to individual selfhood, and this can only be accomplished as a part of the human race.

The truth about the corporate nature of Christian spirituality must be brought into sharp prominence, partly because the devil is afraid of people who set out to engage themselves seriously in the spiritual life. Naturally he uses every device he can to abort that activity. One familiar sophistry starts with the insinuation that the spiritual life is indeed a lonely life; that the call to it is an eccentric vocation to be quite apart at the beginning and to get farther out at the end. "Pious people are weird. A lot of them start out that way; the rest achieve it. But don't just take my word for it. Go down to St. Jude's parish and have an objective look at those neurotics. See if you want to be like that."

Satan slickly bypasses the truth that the Church Militant is more a hospital for sinners than a haven for saints, more a grammar school than a college; but there is enough seeming truth in his words to deceive, if possible, the very elect. If we are seduced by the warning, become convinced of its truth by the examples of certain devotees at St. Jude's, and decide to stay well on this side of "excessive," or "extreme," or "fanatical" involvement—decide, that is to say, just to tip our hats to God on the customary occasions but to avoid any genuine personal relationship with him—the devil can and happily will leave us alone henceforth. On the other hand, if we disregard these hellish hints, the devil has another trick up his sleeve, leading to horrid results at the other extreme. He suggests the flattery that our aloneness is really glorious because we are a superior soul and indeed the only person on the right track. All the others are subhuman and gross.

Once started along this road we speedily become self-righteous, far holier than those benighted clods who probably have no real inkling about genuine spirituality, and who certainly have not entered into the secret places of the Most High as we have. Shortly thereafter we may condescend to foregather with a few other rare souls somewhat like ourselves, although of course not so far advanced, whom we lead off into a corner apart from the church to form a splinter group primarily engaged in admiring its own gnostic splendor. As the Gloomy Dean said, mysticism can so easily begin in mist, center in I, and end in schism.

The devil's sophistry is really a strange one, because in fact it is the secular life that is the lonely one. Since the secular writers themselves amply document this, the point can be ignored here. The present concern is to underline the truth that learning and living the spiritual life is only possible because of the Body of Christ, and in that Body. With the reader's forbearance I have chosen to do so in a personal way, documenting it by means of some realizations that came to mind as I reflected on the topic. My hope here is that my own thankful reminiscences will find a response, suggesting to others the way they themselves have walked, and the company they have kept on the journey. Thus we will be gratefully remembering together our spiritual mother, The Church, and realizing anew the truth of that ancient sentence, "He cannot have God for his Father who does not have the Church for his mother." In so many words, my approach is one of personal reminiscence in my own terms, directed to the personal recollections of others in their terms. That approach necessarily makes for constant use of the first person singular, but in the corporate context it will be recognized as being only a manner of speaking.

Mercifully, I am proposing to single out only three illustrative ways in which the church, through its Head and members, has brought spiritual life to us all.

1.—My beginnings were in my home, and as it were by osmotic process from that basic cell of the church, the family—that microcosm of the Holy Family in which Jesus Himself increased in wisdom and stature and in favor with God and man. Naturally, I have no recollection of being made a member of the human race by birth, nor of being made a member of Christ, the child of God, and an inheritor of the Kingdom of Heaven by baptism. Neither do I have any particular recollection of the early ways of nurture that followed these beginnings. It must suffice to say that our home was simply oriented that way— oriented both in accordance with the "Precepts of Good Citizenship" and with the "Precepts of the Church."

In regard to the latter, the way of life developed across the Christian centuries was thankfully taken for granted and entered into without ostentation or self-consciousness. The Christian Year's ebb and flow—Advent, Christmas, Lent, Easter, Friday, Sunday—guided our family life. Prayer graced our meals, our mornings, and our evenings; sacred symbols graced our walls. Parish clergy were our friends, the Catechism was learned at its proper time, Confirmation released us children from Sunday School to sing in the choir, thereby earning fifty cents a month and the privilege of an annual week at Choir Camp. In short, my parents did not seem to believe it was a good idea to let children grow up in a spiritual vacuum, so that when they became of age they would be able to make a wise free choice in regard to religion.

I have no other recollection of how I learned in the family that human life is God-centered, and that prayer—talking with the living God—is not only possible but absolutely normal and natural. Yet that is what I learned. I do not recall being taught to pray, but obviously I was, far before conscious memory can recall. As one result, to cite a still-vivid memory, when a small crisis occurred in my young life I was not lost or lonely. One night when I may have been about ten years old I fell into an utter panic. I cannot now recall why. I can only remember the enormity of the gripping fear. I was frightened half to death and of course could not sleep. After a few minutes of the horror I slid out of bed, knelt down beside it, talked for a while to my Father in heaven, and then went back to bed. The panic completely vanished, not at all to my surprise, and I fell immediately to sleep.

2.—After those early habits had carried me through the upsets of college, I built on the foundation more systematically in seminary, aided by life among those members of the Body who were my associates there. Some of them, the professorial ones, taught me articulately the rounded faith upon which the spiritual life rests, and which it expresses as well as conveys. Others of them, fellow students, brought me new knowledge of depth and extent. By and large, the more "evangelical" heritage of the church came to me when a few of us began gathering together on Lenten mornings at five o'clock for group prayer and meditation. The more "catholic" tradition came to me through three monks who were my classmates and intimate friends. Through their lives and words they taught me Rule, the basic place of Office and Eucharist in the life of prayer, and the value of sacramental Confession. The whole life in general opened my eyes to a vast treasury of time-tested devotion, including such apparently obvious things as retreats, which I had not so much as heard of until then.

At the center of all was a holy priest in a holy parish full of holy people—a group so anchored in the other world that it was the most powerful social-service force, inch for inch and pound for pound, in New York City. It was my incredible lot to be cast with this wise and saintly priest, this member of the Body who had become holy in that Body, and whom I shortly asked to become my spiritual director in the remote hope that he might be able to pass something of value on to me. Under his direction, my religious life was for several years lived in the midst of the holy parish I have indicated. The prayers of thousands were steeped into the very walls of their church. The supernatural was tangibly around. Anyone could feel the power of the place, radiating from the vitality of the members of the Body who had gone before and who were presently there. The result was a genuine House of God, compellingly conducive to the spiritual life.

3.—After this firm grounding in good habits, sound doctrine, wide vision, and personal inspiration—wrought through individual skill and patience in the mutual support of a corporate life—I "went out on my own," of course continuing the solid life of worship, prayer, and discipline in the Communion of Saints. In this life still other individual members of Christ's Body came, and are still coming, to my aid. Some of these were people like Fr. Huntington, Fr. Hughson, and Fr. Joseph, to cite three monastic priests whose names everyone knows, and who can represent a dozen others of less fame but equal wisdom who led me deeper into the spiritual life. Others were folk—some of them steady companions, others, ships that passed in the night with a most welcome hail— unknown to anyone but myself and God, but who have counterparts in everyone's experience, for God has left none of us without these contemporary witnesses in the Body of Christ who help us so much.

Neither has He left us without the immeasurable aid of those other members of the Body who are not in the Church Militant any more, but from whom a singular vitality flows to all the other members. In illustration I will single out again only those articulate members of the Communion of Saints whose works so tangibly live after them—the spiritual writers of all the centuries, without whom we would be lost and floundering.

In some such manner as that sketched above, each of us made his beginnings and continuings in the spiritual life. We grow Godward because of personal involvement in the corporate life of the church, much as a marine recruit becomes a real marine by living in the Marine Corps.

Having presented the obverse of this matter, we must now turn the coin over and at least glance at some important features on its reverse. Lamentably, at no time in the history of the earthly Church Militant, that small visible part of the Body of Christ that so dimly reflects The Church Triumphant in heaven, does it remain wholly faithful to its Founder and Head, its scriptures, its tradition. Occasionally it scrapes actual bottom and resembles Antichrist. At other times, as in our own era, the church simply does not seem to amount to anything much, except perhaps a tower of Babel. The responsibility for such a dreadful situation of course resides primarily with the earthly leadership of the church to whom its welfare has been entrusted. The pressure of it, however, falls upon the dedicated individual churchman. What can he do, what should he do, when in all honesty, in vast sorrow unmixed with anger or rancor, with self-righteousness and rationalization not in point, he feels in the church like an illegitimate child at a family reunion?

The more devoted a churchman is, the more exquisite is his dilemma. He realizes that he learned in and from the church the very standards by which he is judging the church. He knows that he owes his own developed and still developing selfhood, together with that most important factor his *sense* of his own selfhood, to the church. He is also persuaded that it is not enough for selves just to stand there, even if they stand for something; they must actively repay their debt. They must be committed *to* something, lest their hardly won integrity and identity suffer erosion.

A higher, less selfish level of the same truth is that the world constantly needs people who are true to themselves, and who are always in short supply.

Lacking such, and the church which produces them, the world also would erode, crumble, and ultimately collapse. Of course for a while it would coast along in neutral, getting somewhere before slowing to a stop. For a time it could live off its own stored fat before it starved to death. For a season the flowers that are Standards—Principles—Morality—would continue to bloom after being severed from their nourishing roots in religion. But this is only for a season.

And on a still higher level, an additional problem arises because a dedicated churchman views the church not just as a means to an end but as an end—*the* End—in itself. He considers it to be The Body of Christ, struggling and battered here on earth, to be sure, but at the same time reigning triumphantly and eternally in heaven. "Wilt thou also go away?", to him, has only one possible answer. There is no place to go, here or hereafter.

Caught in this dilemma, equally unable to drop out of or to remain within the church of his day, should a churchman keep especially in mind that Christ warned against following false prophets and told the lukewarm Laodicean church He would spew it out of His mouth, or should he dwell on the truth that "Christ loved the church and gave himself for it"? History records that both roads diverging at this fork have been heavily traveled. Some troubled souls have elected separation from the decadent Church Militant of their miserable eras. Others have constituted themselves a loyal opposition within it. We will find heroes on whichever course we follow in obedience to our own acquired integrity at that time. St. Athanasius, St. Francis of Assisi, St. Thomas More, Martin Luther, the Wesleys, John Keble, and a million others went one way or the other and forever shine like stars in the particular darkness of their time. I know a hundred otherwise unknown ones sparkling in our own night, and so do you.

We know another thing, too: both courses involve personal suffering, frequently to the extreme of actual martyrdom. In order that our decision become a fruitful and healing one, we have to join Christ on His redeeming cross—He was on this very mission—and stay there, in our too few better moments praying that nails and rope will hold us fast, prevailing even against our own impatience, impotence, and despair. "Without shedding of blood is no remission."

The positive side of this truth is that "the blood of the martyrs is the seed of the church." God works His most typical miracles when all conditions of success are nonexistent, but personal faith holds firm nonetheless. Abraham believed and had a son when Sarah was long past childbearing age. Jesus came into the world when Mary had to say "How shall this be?" Christ accepted death even though it was incredible that a dead king could bring in a kingdom. Whatever we do, we must abide in faith and patience, waiting for the moving of the waters. While we continue in faithful suffering and prayer, God is preparing such a solution for our present impossibility as we ourselves cannot even imagine.

Chapter Ten

Liturgy

AT THE CENTER of the church's corporate life, at the center of its vast all-embracing activity by which time and space are sanctified, is liturgy, public worship. The heart of liturgy is the Holy Eucharist. Because the Eucharist occupies that position in the life of the Church, inevitably it does the same in the life of a churchman.

Because it does, nothing sufficient can be said about the Eucharist. Oceans of words, seas of books, rivers of hymns and other devotions have poured forth on the subject, and yet endless possibility remains. We have here an instance of the classic gap between the infinite and the finite. All the grains of sand on the shores of all the seas are no closer in number to infinity than is a single grain. So if only one overview of the Eucharist is herein suggested as being spiritually fruitful, let that be taken as merely one approach among many. Furthermore, let it be clear that our approach will view the Eucharist more from a devotional angle than from that of an objective liturgist.

Nevertheless, something must be said in general preamble about liturgy, the church's most proper work and the only aspect of the Eucharist under consideration in the present chapter that continues our discussion of corporate prayer. Other valid and precious facets of the Eucharist, expressed in such titles as "Holy Communion" or "The Lord's Supper," will be considered separately and later.

Liturgy is an action; is something done, and done corporately. It is an offering to God the Father by God the Son—by Christ in His new body the church, through which He remains operative in the world. Because we are in Christ; because we are members of His body; it is an action offered to God the Father by us.

By no means is it addressed *to* us. We do not attend the liturgy primarily to listen individually to the service or the sermon or the music, hoping to profit therefrom. Essentially, we go as working members of a body and to give rather than to get. Hence no celebrant declaims the liturgy as if it had earthly hearers or uses ceremony to be impressing. There is no one present to be impressed. All have gathered into one in order to *express*. No one is watching as from a grandstand. Everyone is on the field of action, engaged together "with angels and archangels, and with all the company of heaven" in offering a corporate action to the one God and Father of all. At the conclusion of the liturgy we can easily be wearied by the outpouring, somewhat as our Lord was exhausted (and fulfilled) at the completion of His life on earth in a physical body.

There are many good ways in which we may engage ourselves in the corporate action. Some will shortly be suggested here. Regardless of the way we find most congenial, we should arrive at the place of offering early, eager, and ready, after care and thought taken the night before. Furthermore, the discipline of silence looms large in the work, for it tends to check a merely horizontal, or social, directedness. Liturgy's orientation is vertical. Idle chatter in church or curious staring about obviously pulls at least two people back to earth. Indeed, liturgical prayer is no occasion for asserting one's own individuality but for merging oneself into the Body of Christ. In expressive symbol, when specialized members of the one Body—choir, acolytes, clergy—enter, the rest of the members weld everything into one by standing. The congregation does not rise to sing a hymn, or to honor the priest, or even to honor the priesthood of Christ. The point of the symbol is that the Body of Christ, now present in all His members at a particular time and place, girds itself and stands united to be about His work.

Some fruitful ways in which we may do so stem from viewing the Holy Eucharist as the life of our Lord—once lived on earth in a human body in which He did many mighty words, especially including His blessed passion and precious death, His mighty resurrection and glorious ascension—now being re-presented to God the Father in His new body. The same activities undertaken over the course of some thirty years so long ago in Palestine may be seen as now being offered in some sixty minutes through the Eucharist. Some familiar—especially to Anglicans, Lutherans, Roman Catholics, the Orthodox, *et al*—illustrative parallels can be quickly sketched.

From the start of the Eucharist through the Kyries we can think of the liturgy as reenacting the preparation of the world, and the world's responsive yearning for the coming of God the Son into it at the appointed time. In a few minutes, from Introit to Kyrie, we are reliving the thousands of years from the Fall of Man to the first Christmas, when the Son came to His beloved world to redeem it and set it straight again by pointing it in perfect obedience to the Father.

The Gloria in Excelsis, that song of the Angels at the first Christmas, which occurs in liturgy immediately after the final expectant Kyrie, is of course, in this rationale, the birth of Christ.

There follows, in Epistle, Gospel, sermon, and Creed our Lord's teaching ministry in which He mediated God to man by declaring truth. In the liturgy He thus continues to bring divine light into uncomprehending darkness, as He did on so many occasions in so many spoken ways in the days of His flesh.

His work of intercession in specific prayers, done on earth so often in His physical body, obviously is entered into by His mystical body at the liturgical Great Intercession.

The frequent "mystical moments" in His earthly life, such as the Transfiguration, are expressed liturgically in the Sanctus, which relives those occasions when the veil that separates this world from that was parted, and we are visibly at one with the company of heaven.

The reorientation of the world toward its proper end occurs at the Offertory and, in Him who did it first and sufficiently, supremely in the Prayer of Consecration. Here the single purpose of Christ's life—summed up in that "Lo, I come to do Thy will, O God"—shows clearly. Here is Holy Week, beginning with the Palm Sunday entrance, continuing through the Last Supper and the Crucifixion, finally climaxing in the Resurrection. The culmination of it all in the Ascension, when in His last earthly act Jesus blessed His disciples as His human body finally left them and they returned to Jerusalem, is of course represented at the dismissal and blessing. Just as the original disciples then returned to Jerusalem—to the world, where in the power of the Holy Spirit they would continue His mighty acts until His coming again—so do we then depart, in the same power and on the same mission.

The Eucharist viewed thus is the life of Christ reoffered to God the Father in our day. In the mystery of time and eternity it is Jesus offering His full redeeming life to the Father, not long ago and far away but in our own parish church right now. In the mystery of our sacramental incorporation into Him, it is ourselves in Him confronting the Father on behalf of the world.

In sum, when involved in the Eucharist we are involved with our Lord's eternal life. We are caught up into the activity of His Real Presence, rather than a mere remembrance of His real absence.

The first of three suggested ways to take effective part in that mighty work is especially suited to those whose typical prayer is "Vocal." Of course our disciplined bodies, expressing their spirits, engage themselves in the customary ways of suiting the action to the word—in standing, sitting, kneeling they are "vocal" too. Our minds also involve themselves in the literal rite with the closest possible attention. With Prayer Book in hand or with the familiar words in memory, we offer thanksgiving when our Lord is doing that; praise when He is thus engaged; intercession when the church turns to that work. We steadfastly refuse to offer penitence when the church is engaged in adoration, even if penitence is our individual mood at the moment. We are well aware that liturgy is corporate, not private prayer, and so in the corporate prayer we do what the body wants done at the moment. We take our purposeful part in the group action, not seeking to impose an individual will upon the team but, quite properly, doing things the other way around.

Naturally this is most easily done by rather slavishly following the action being prescribed at the time. Obviously such attention helps strongly to keep us precisely with the church. Sometimes, when the self is particularly dull, all it can really offer is a pedestrian loyalty, almost continually distracted by impatience that the chore be finished. On better days, however, we bring a far more vital member to the work of the body. With individual vocal prayer we particularize the necessarily generalized rite in the liturgy. For example, when the church is interceding for her clergy, we privately insert the Christian names of those in the area of our responsibility and love. When the corporate intention centers on the sick, we are ready with individuals to include. When our Lord's mind is concerned with souls in the next world, we go with Him there and pray especially for this Richard, or that Mary, with whom it had pleased Him to cast our lot on earth.

Perhaps we remember how we learned this privilege and duty as children, possibly at an Instructed Eucharist when time and guidance were given to the matter. Perhaps we had been brought up in a parish where, on occasion, a basket was passed at this time, and we placed on it a list of names we had prepared in advance. It may be that we ourselves had sometimes been chosen to carry this collection to the celebrant, who set it before God on the altar. Regardless of how the knowledge had come home to us, we realize that God has put us where we are, to be His hands and feet and heart in that place. Loyally or fervently, we carry out the responsibility in corporate prayer, particularizing the general offering in accordance with its varying moods of thanksgiving, penitence, praise, and all the rest. Experience has taught us that we cannot come empty-handed and vacant-minded to the offering, presuming that in the course of things we will be moved to do a stroke or two of real work. The action is too swift for that. It will have moved on to another subject before we can take time to think. So we collect our thoughts in advance, and come prepared to exercise our membership in the body.

Discussion of another way to offer the liturgy requires a brief reminder of what a "votive" Eucharist is. In a sense every celebration is a "votive"—that is to say, is especially devoted to an individual element in the total life of Christ. The Eucharist of course remains His total life, but nevertheless each offering singles out for special attention a particular aspect, part, or emphasis in that life.

The Christian Year does exactly this, for example. The Christmas Eucharist, in celebrating the whole life of our Lord from birth to ascension, devotes its center of attention to the mystery of the Incarnation. The Easter Eucharist is devoted especially to the Resurrection; its hymns, other propers, and general mood concentrate on one great fact in the whole. Even the Sundays after Pentecost have an individual "mind," with each one emphasizing a particular facet of the total teaching of Christ. Each is devoted to its own, with individual

"Propers" accenting the "Ordinary." Each is a "votive," a particularization, adapted to the fact of our limited and particularizing minds.

The observance of Saints' Days uses the same principle. All Saints' Day is of course devoted to honoring God for the whole membership in the Communion of Saints. Nevertheless, each individual saint's day centers our attention on a particular person—exactly as birthday celebrations do in the yearly round of family life in an individual home.

In final illustration, the church uses still other ways to accent one aspect of our Lord's total life. At an ordination, or a nuptial Eucharist, or a requiem, it especially relives with Him these individual parts of the whole. The votive Eucharist devotes its attention, its intention, and its power to the action of the moment.

An individual member of Christ's Body is privileged to do exactly the same. As a matter of practical fact, probably none of us ever offers the Eucharist without at least a vague "special intention"—a cause or concern in life that we want to incorporate in our Lord and hold up in Him before the Father. Indeed, sometimes the "special intention" is the only real way we can take part in the action. In times of great concern, such as an overwhelming sorrow that completely dominates us, the best we can do (in a double sense of the phrase) is just hold it there, perhaps quite numbly, in Christ.

Every parish priest has innumerable requests for these special intentions or offers them unasked because he knows something of what is in the hearts and on the minds of his parishioners. Beyond that, in wide parochial practice throughout the church—especially where the daily Eucharist is the norm— every day is a votive. Every day is devoted to a special intention, either because of the church's mandate on, say, the Feast of the Transfiguration, or the celebrant's choice, or by another individual's request. Day after day finds the offering of a requiem, or a votive for the sick, or one for those traveling, or one of thanksgiving, or of the Holy Spirit for inspiration and guidance, and so on *ad infinitum*. The church has developed these votives for use in all the changes and chances of this mortal life.

The present pratical point is that we are privileged not merely to offer our own special intentions, as they emerge in life through "the regular parish Eucharist," but that we have additional right and even responsibility to request that our own desired votive be the parish offering on a stated day. For complete clarity it must be interjected here that on occasion it is not possible to honor such a request on a particular day. When the mind of the whole church is devoted to a matter, that must take precedence of any individual mind. In example, a requiem cannot be offered on Easter Day—nor can any other substitution then be made, for that matter. The individual request is transferred to the first available open day, just as occasionally happens in the Church Year itself. (The unfortunate saints whose days occur in late Lent are continually having their birthday celebrations moved about.)

Usually, however, a desired day is readily available for votive purposes. The habit of letting our requests, or our thanks, be made known to God in this special way greatly sanctifies space and time, both for ourselves and for others. By it, religion takes on life, and life takes on religion. We walk through life with our Lord, just as was done in those historic days when people laid the sick or the dead before Him or in any way touched the hem of His garment.

Still another excellent manner of individual involvement in corporate prayer is by way of praying in union with the varying moods of the Eucharist. Obviously this cannot be used by a sheer beginner, for only familiarity can make one fluidly aware of what those moods are. Fairly soon, however, we do arrive at the point when we know what our Lord is going to do next. If, in addition to that, our characteristic prayer is affective, we can work well with Him in such a manner.

To take an illustration, during the entire Introit-Kyrie action one might well offer prayers in keeping with the then prevailing mood of preparation. These might be acts of thanksgiving for the work of the Holy Spirit in the world at large and in ourselves in the small. They might include a longing that the work be further extended in ourselves and in others. They could take the form of aspiration for the fulfillment of the whole process.

In further example, during the Epistle and Gospel one would not need to pay direct attention to the words themselves, as perhaps one used to do in the days before meditation had imprinted these in the fiber of one's being, or when vocal prayer prevailed. Participation could well, and probably better, be done through thanksgiving for The Word Who came into the world, and to us, and to me. One might then naturally slide into petition and intercession that we, and I, may hear Him more clearly, love Him more dearly, follow Him more nearly. There could just as well be fervent aspiration for the success of the church's mission—or for particular "teaching" parts of it like the seminaries.

In final suggestion, during the Consecration (possibly we make a menal image of the table of the Last Supper, with Calvary superimposed upon it) the prayer might most fittingly be adoration of the Sacrifice, or identification with the divine self-giving, or praise for its benefits, or offering of the Church Militant in union with the oblation.

Engaging in the liturgy in that manner—praying it affectively—is more often than not a work of joy to the point of being a lot of fun. One can only guess at the liturgical delights savored by those whose way of prayer is contemplation.

The primary reasons for plunging deeply into the corporate life and work of the church—the glory of God, the strengthening of His church, and the presentation of His world to Him in Jesus—need no further underscoring here. On the other hand, it may be well to mention a secondary benefit to ourselves.

In a former chapter it was indicated that prayer brings us to the heart meaning of doctrine as nothing else can. The intimate connection between Christian Cult and Christian education has also been sketched, or at least hinted, herein. We can restate these truths now, in swift technical language, by saying that ascetics is the essential middle term between doctrine and morals. The same thought can be translated into Biblical terms by the important statement that the Truth issues into the Life only by means of our going the Way. There is no method, other than living the spiritual life in the Body of Christ, by which we can really comprehend what the church is saying. The bearing of that fact on Christian education in general, which the reader was asked to keep in mind, is obvious.

The bearing of our point upon "the moral life" is closer to the thesis of this book: there is no way, other than through the spiritual life, by which Christian teaching can become Christian living. In ridiculous illustration, let us imagine a track coach who gathers his aspirants for Olympic glory and holds high standards before them. "I expect you to run the hundred in ten seconds, to pole-vault eighteen feet, to long-jump twenty-nine feet." Having thus exhorted his charges, the coach ends his work for the season and goes home to smoke his pipe in slippered ease.

Although the standards are important enough, nevertheless the coach will shortly be fired, of course, because his real job is not to hold up standards but to make their attainment possible. His own brand of strenuous ascetics—training table and training methods—must be applied before what he says can issue in what his disciples do.

The present point is that when we are dealing with liturgy we are involved with *lex orandi lex credendi*—with the faith of the church expressed in its official prayer. The church prays in accordance with its beliefs, and as one consquence of our taking these enormous truths, devotionally expressed, upon our lips and into our hearts, they tend to take up real lodging in the depths of our being, issuing thence in real living.

Through living immersion in the total faith totally expressed, we come really to know the true standards; we increase in knowledge of what Christ's mind really is. We are prevented from going disastrously off the rails into always impoverishing heresy—there is indeed such a thing as heresy, and it is indeed always less than the best. *Lex orandi lex credendi* keep us from settling for running the hundred in a mere twelve seconds.

The passing years of corporate involvement also immensely enable our ability to approach, even ultimately to attain, the coach's ten-second goal. We will be alluding to both of these matters again in the next chapter, along with many other things.

Chapter Eleven

Daily Offering and Communion

THE JOY OF the weekday Eucharist begins on the physical plane. You are up and out at an early hour, walking or driving down quiet streets. On especially alert days, particularly if you are walking, you can be sensibly part of a world off to a fresh start.

Winter or summer, Maine or Mississippi, city or country—these variables do not seem to make much difference in this regard. I remember driving to church with the sunshine slanting through the Florida trees, urging them to life and stirring up their birds and squirrels before flashing on to dance with the river. With the same overtones I also remember, across many years, the solid clop of heavy horses' hooves as they drew milkwagons over New York City cobblestones on frigid winter mornings, when the wind off the Hudson bit hard as I walked two frozen miles through the darkness to attend early Eucharist in the seminary chapel.

To meet God sacramentally is, however, to find His presence less veiled than it is through the revelations of nature. The passage through nature, down city street or rural road, really serves as distant preparation for this genuine meeting. The church building itself, if its artists have done a sensitive job, affords more intimate preparation. Especially in the early morning a church seems a tangible bridge between two worlds—the one you are passing through, and the one you are heading toward. It is dim and quiet, pleasantly cool or warm— whichever is required to compensate for the weather outside the doors now shut behind you. In closing those doors you haven't shut the world away, you realize. Rather, you are carrying its essentials across a bridge leading to the true end. Moving toward the candlelight flickering on silver and brass at the altar end, you sense that you have not so much entered a sanctuary apart from this world as you have opened the antechamber to another world which edges into, merges with, this one. Exactly as you brought the natural world here with you, just so will the supernatural world bring its eternities to you.

You kneel in a familiar pew, finding satisfaction in being able to start the day with recollection, with awareness, with a sense of purpose and direction, with the knowledge of first things put first. Once again you are glad of your resolution, made long ago, to keep alive the sense of God by constant reexposure in this manner. God doesn't need it, but you do. Just living in the world with all its legitimate pressures lays one open to spiritual erosion.

As in your pew you begin to become part of the vital stillness you say a few slow, easy, accustomed personal prayers, doubtless realizing once again that lack of private prayer involves loss of personal identity and that you had better pull yourself up in this department. With the others present you join in the preparatory corporate office of Matins, perhaps noting that neglected corporate prayer takes its toll in loss of balance and vision. You make an appropriate resolution. Then these good, but self-regarding thoughts drop away, and the sheerly spiritual side takes over. As prepared as you can be, you go unto the altar of God where a two-sided activity is under way—the activity of offering and of receiving.

It is said that the world needs spiritual energy. It is said that our greatest single need is for spiritual and moral power that proceeds from and produces spiritual and moral awakening. Too seldom, however, are we told *how* to be spiritually awake, or how to provide spiritual power for a sick world's needs. Hence, "What can I do?" is so frequently the earnest individual's cry. What can I do in the midst of clashing civilizations, in materialism run rampant, in corruption and conniving in high places, in sickness and despair, in fears and worries? Participating in, hence beset by the world, what can one small individual do to make himself count eternally?

One most definite thing that can be done is to offer the once-for-all sacrifice of Christ on Calvary frequently, even daily, at the church's altar. As you kneel there sharing in the offering of God the Son—with the whole world in His arms—to God the Father, you join a never ending offering by other priests and people all over the world in village chapels and city churches. Countless hearts in many nations are pouring prayer and aspiration upward, as they hold the redeeming Son before the omnipotent Father once more, and yet eternally, on behalf of the race of men.

"Look, Father, look on His anointed face and only look on us as found in Him," they pray. "Between our sins and their reward, we set the passion of Thy son our Lord . . . . By this prevailing Presence we appeal. O do Thine utmost for their souls' true weal."

The world needs Christ? The world *has* Christ, quietly yet powerfully at work all the days of eternity in the Eucharist. Here is genuine spiritual power of the highest order—the Holy Eucharist is omnipotence in prayer. Here, then, is one thing we can do. We can hold the Son before the Father in our day, linking ourselves with Him, merging our causes with His.

An incredible freight goes up there at the altar in, with, and under the familiar words that are new every morning. People sick and in the hospital, slaves to evil habits, worried and fearful folk, departed souls, those needing guidance, our bishops and other clergy, our racial tensions, our young people, our old people, our statesmen and our politicians—everyone and everything we can think of, and many more things that we have not yet discerned, are held before the Father, in the Son, every day at altars throughout the world. More things are asked in prayer and are wrought by the tremendous intercession of our Lord—Head and members—in the Eucharist than this world dreams of.

There are, thanks be to God, vast numbers who do know how and where to take burdens and place them securely, offering them in confidence of God's sure blessing on them. By their action the things of space and time are made holy as the world of nature is held high.

In the providing of God, all this turns around and comes toward us; the other world stoops to this one, sanctifying it from above. With one proviso. Christ wills to walk about His world again this day—every day—but He wills to do so in us His members, tabernacling there by means of a piece of consecrated bread. When this appointment meets response, He will go to His world.

And thus *we* are able to go. Not only for those others, but for us also there is unmeasured need. There is so much going out of us, draining out of us. There is so much physical, nervous, mental, and spiritual strength going out, draining away every day. So much is demanded of us, with the demands ever increasing; with the needs piling up precisely as our own unaided resources to meet them begin to fail. For these daily needs we must have daily bread; where shall we find it? At the Holy Table of God, of course, which He provided so that He could give us unfailing strength for continuing work. In the power of this bread we can go our own full journey into the wilderness, doing all the necessary things of God through God who strengthens us for them.

"How can you—in addition to all the things you are already doing every day—how can you take on this extra duty?" Precisely because of these responsibilities, how can you not?

Offering and receiving—the divine give-and-take is available most tangibly at the early weekday Eucharist. We enter this world, we make this contribution, we receive these gifts, quite simply—as simply as beginning the habit of attending a weekday Eucharist.

Like all habits, the habit of the daily Eucharist is attained in the doing of it—by starting it and keeping it up. It is as simple as selecting an hour, and going with alert body, mind, and soul through the world, into the church, to the altar table of God, and back out into the world again.

Chapter Twelve

Intercession

TO US CHRISTIANS the fact is clear that God entered this world to bring us to ourselves by bringing us to Himself. The record is clear that as our blessed Lord moved about His fallen world on this mission, He sought out and dispelled evil in many particular forms. He entered here and entered there, bringing redeeming love into wretched situations—forgiving, healing, answering, feeding, restoring, raising, delivering, bringing harmony. However, as we study His trail we note that, in addition to the print of active feet, we find in it the deeper imprint of knees—and at the end a trace of blood. We observe that the marks of the knees are often seen in the midst of the action itself, but that more frequently they are found off to the side where their maker withdrew for a while to labor from this posture alone. We get the impression that here He was dispelling evil in general.

In plain surface words, the divine way of entering into, repairing, and ennobling the human situation is two-dimensional, empowering the "intercession of social action" with the "intercession of prayer."

More fundamentally expressed, the divine method was and is to bring the supernatural to bear upon the natural by lifting the natural up into the supernatural. American Christianity, chronically in danger of degenerating into a mere social gospel of good works, constantly needs reminding of this divine method and especially needs reminding of prayer's priority in the mind and work of Christ. In words, our Lord told us that certain situations yield only to prayer and fasting (which indicates why these situations always persist, even in the greatest secular society). In events, on the night in which He was betrayed our Lord did not rush out into that darkness to heal a few last sick ones. Instead, He used His precious time to gather up the whole world and offer it in intercession to His Father. The next day He let them immobilize His ministering hands and feet and from this straitened posture made the complete intercession of Himself for the world.

His work does not end there, in drops of blood. The resurrection and ascension lift spiritual sight, bringing knowledge that even the crucifixion was not Christ's final intercession. The ultimate truth is that our Lord still and always pleads our human needs before the Father. The "Intercessor, Friend of sinners, earth's Redeemer" came into the world, participated deeply in it, and continues to carry its burdens eternally. He is doing so at this moment, thereby making fruitful all we attempt to do in Him—"Greater works than these shall (ye) do; because I go unto my Father."

The words "intercessor" and "intercession" have been introduced here in this final chapter as vigorous synonyms for "the spiritual life", because through this awkward translation our thesis may become clearer—that the mediative and energizing powers of spirituality break through into the natural world, bringing sure knowledge, deft touch, and impressive strength. In thus reiterating the Christian conviction that what is beyond nature makes its will and power felt and known in nature through spirit-filled people, there is obviously no disparagement of social action. There is no such disparagement even in our presently saying that social service will always have its devotees and practitioners. On the contrary, this service is part of "intercession" and comes from God, if not always straight from Him. As a matter of fact it is a glorious commentary on the reality of love that almost everyone, even the agnostic, learns and practices some compassion from living in the world. However, we are more concerned here with Christians, the true salt of the earth, who learn something vastly more than physical compassion from living in the church.

In one hyphenated word, the Christian there learns adoration-intercession, and we have taken pains to indicate that he can learn that in no other milieu. In fact, the church is God's deliberate creation for this purpose. By baptism a Christian is above all things moved over into the supernatural world, incorporated into Christ, and becomes potentially an adorer-intercessor. Called by baptism to "worship God; and to work and pray and give" for His kingdom, he is ever afterwards instructed in this life by the church which is by no means merely *like* the life of Christ. It *is* the life of Christ today. Adoration-intercession is learned by living in Him who is this personified. Here is the church's true work, or life, to which it must remain true—primarily for God's glory, but also because if it doesn't the world will collapse.

We repeat that primarily we learn the Christian life of adoration-intercession at the altar, that reoffering of Calvary in our day and the *raison d'etre* of corporate Christian life. Here our Lord is lifted up and men look upon Him in adoration. Here our Lord offers Himself daily on behalf of the world's needs. And here we adore and intercede in His body, thus learning to do so according to the mind of our Lord rather than according to the mere guidance and fervency of our own limited insights and moods.

At first, undoubtedly, those latter items, which are so understandably in the forefront of our awareness, will dominate our practice. That isn't too bad. Intercession—by which, again, is here meant the full spiritual life—expresses and releases us, so by it we do "feel better." In it, we know with peculiar certainty and satisfaction that we are vitally part of the creation that groans and travails together. Furthermore, it is no incidental to be scorned that intercession contributes to our total development—that we ourselves grow deeply as its steady practice proceeds. As always is the case when talents are exercised, the creative work of spiritual involvement does greatly benefit the participants. Yet the neophyte intercessor, continually immersed in the life and mind of the church, soon moves beyond this. Shortly he learns the basic truth that intercession is work to be done rather than emotion to be felt. In time he senses the mystic truth that we, Christ's members, live to join Him in His steady labor, each offering in Him the particular concerns with which we have been entrusted, and that thus the high-priestly prayer and work never end, even on earth. Finally he comes to see the utter primacy of the spiritual.

When he reaches this point, the individual intercessor can then with safety begin to free-lance. Inevitably he will, as he learns ever more and more from the church what it means to have been incorporated into Christ. Some of these members of Christ may discover the specialized vocation of enclosed intercessor, which the Church perennially needs—perhaps never more than in our secular day. In most cases, however, they will begin to move about the world as intercessors, in good works always but increasingly in the intercession of prayer. They will, indeed, come to the time when they never approach a problem, or a task, or human contact, nor leave it, without a prayer that what they say and do, or leave unsaid or undone, will be as God wills. Beyond that, they will see voids, glaring gaps, and will move in to fill them—they will create, not merely react. They will see intercession, both in work and prayer, as being the offering of their total selves for God to take and use for His real and abiding purposes.

No one has yet solved the problem of the interaction of God's omnipotence and human free will, but the practical way this mystery works is perfectly illustrated in the Feeding of the Multitudes—in the "whence shall we buy bread, that these may eat?" although "he himself knew what he would do." God has so ordered the world that we share in creative power with Him. He wants the hungry fed, but we have to organize and administer the United Fund. He wants truth known, but scientists and teachers are not irrelevant. He wants eternal souls brought into being, but even here He works through the cooperation of human parents. God's work is always furthered or frustrated by the right or wrong use of our energy. Herein, surely, is the true rationale of our intercession. It isn't that God doesn't know the world's needs, or doesn't care about them, or won't bestir Himself unless He is prodded. The point is not God's reluctance—we know better than that—but our availability for His use. It is only when creative contact is made between God and man that power flows.

We are saying once again that, far from removing us from the world into an ivory tower, the spiritual life fills and opens the mind, the heart, the time, and the strength on behalf of the world. Unavoidably it does so because immersion in Christ leads to continuing growth of Christ in us, and these things characterize Him.

The first observable result of this union is personal—it builds a self worthy of the name. As grace flows through, we ourselves become ever more graceful. But over and above that is the greater truth. By the spiritual life, by adoration-intercession, heaven and earth are joined in the manner God intended they should be. The one flows into the other. The redemptive process advances as nature is penetrated by supernature and lifted above itself. God the continuing creator, having found and widened a channel in man, floods with power and ever more power through that man into the whole race of men.

64297 First Printing March